ONE SIGNAL
PUBLISHERS

ATRIA

Also by Reshma Saujani

Brave, Not Perfect

Pay Up

THE FUTURE OF
WOMEN
AND WORK

(and Why It's Different
Than You Think)

Reshma Saujani

ONE SIGNAL
PUBLISHERS

ATRIA

New York · London · Toronto · Sydney · New Delhi

ONE SIGNAL
PUBLISHERS

ATRIA

An Imprint of Simon & Schuster, Inc.
1230 Avenue of the Americas
New York, NY 10020

First One Signal Publishers/Atria Books hardcover edition March 2022

ONE SIGNAL PUBLISHERS / ATRIA BOOKS and colophon are
trademarks of Simon & Schuster, Inc.

For information about special discounts for bulk purchases,
please contact Simon & Schuster Special Sales at 1-866-506-1949 or
business@simonandschuster.com.

The Simon & Schuster Speakers Bureau can bring authors to your live event.
For more information or to book an event, contact the Simon & Schuster
Speakers Bureau at 1-866-248-3049 or visit our website at www.simonspeakers.com.

Interior design by Dana Sloan

Manufactured in the United States of America

1 3 5 7 9 10 8 6 4 2

Library of Congress Cataloging-in-Publication Data has been applied for.

ISBN 978-1-9821-9157-3
ISBN 978-1-9821-9159-7 (ebook)

For the next generation of women, so the workplace of the future finally works for them

Contents

PROLOGUE

The Big Lie

I did everything right.

Like many women in America, I'd always wanted a big career. And kids. And a rich family life that would look and feel joyful and fulfilling. As the daughter of immigrant parents who believed wholeheartedly in the promise of the American Dream, I wanted it all and believed without a shred of doubt that I could have it.

To get there, I hit all the prescribed stepping-stones. In school I studied hard to get straight As and become number one on the debate team so I could get into a top college. Once in college, I worked even harder to be valedictorian so I could get into a top law school and land a job at a prestigious law firm, even though I secretly dreamed of being in public service. The plan worked, and I was on my way.

I hated my job, but I never let that show. I figured if I just worked harder, I would get to the next level and I'd be happy. I then moved on to a high-paying job at a renowned financial firm. I hated that, too—the hours were soul-sucking. But still, every day I put on another version of a tastefully tailored Theory suit, squeezed my feet into killer stilettos, and click-clacked my way through the marble lobby and up to my office on the forty-second floor because I was on the "right track" to scale the highest mountains in corporate America.

I took cues from my older male colleagues, the ones whose successes I envied. They had stay-at-home wives who kept their families discreetly (and effortlessly) tucked away, so I did the same. Even though I didn't have kids yet, I desperately wanted to and was obsessed with my niece Maya as if she were my own. At home I plastered my apartment with pictures of my niece but kept only one discreetly pinned up behind my desk at work. My thinking at the time was right in line with the feminist rhetoric that promised if I achieved equality at work, I'd then be on equal footing with the successful men I admired. Of course, the feminist promise overlooked one glaring problem: There would be no stay-at-home partner keeping my family life humming along smoothly and quietly in the background.

By the time I hit my early thirties, I was so sick and miserable that I knew I needed to make a change. To make a long story short, I woke up one day and realized I'd abandoned my dream of making a real difference in the world. This epiphany was startling, empowering, and terrifying all at the same time.

I eventually quit and became the first Indian American woman to run for Congress in New York City. I was thrilled when CNBC touted my race as one of the hottest in the country and I scored endorsements from the *New York Observer* and the *New York Daily News*. This was it! This was the next "right" move—I was supposed to adhere to the well-touted career advice of FOLLOWING MY DREAM!

I lost *spectacularly*, which hurt like hell. After hiding out for a short while to nurse my wounds, I picked myself back up and started to contemplate what was next for me. My thoughts turned to all the classrooms around the city I'd visited while campaigning, where I'd noticed that the coding and robotics labs were notably devoid of girls. It was no wonder that only eighteen percent of the fast-growing, high-paying tech sector jobs were filled by women! I realized that creating gender parity in technology by reaching girls at an early age was how I could still be of service in the big way I dreamed. Start-up entrepreneur: THAT was my next calling on the way to having it all! In 2012, I founded Girls Who Code, to close the gender gap in the technology workforce.

Launching a start-up is a 24/7 endeavor. I was used to working insane hours in law and finance, so for me, taking a non-profit job was not about scaling back or finding balance. It was the exact opposite, and I was thrilled by the challenge. In the early years, I never worked harder or loved a job more. Being the founder and CEO of Girls Who Code gave me, for the first time, the opportunity to preach what I'd been taught was the feminist credo: Equality means equality in the workplace. Better access to jobs would naturally lead to bigger professional opportunities and better lives for our generation of women and generations of women to come.

For a while, it was a perfect fit. I became a relentless cheerleader for getting more women into the tech workforce. Despite the fact that I wasn't a coder and had no experience in the field, or in nonprofit management, I canvassed all the smart people I could get an interview with in the tech sector, in women's education, and in workforce development in order to come up with a six-part plan:

1. Help women get the coding skills they need to land a job in the lucrative tech field.
2. Once they get hired, help them storm the C-suites.
3. Women in tech experiencing a high turnover? We'll keep them motivated by mentoring girls.
4. More women's leadership programs, too. My smart, savvy, talented young women from Girls Who Code wouldn't stop until upper management is largely female. They wouldn't stop till every Mark Zuckerberg was a woman.
5. Keep pushing until at least half the venture capital (VC) money in Silicon Valley is going to women-led companies.
6. Yeah, yeah, yeah! Women hold up half the sky. But we're not going to stop until they also take up half the seats in every corporate boardroom in America!

Everywhere I went, I shouted out this exhilarating message. Infiltrate the boardroom, take it all over!! My voice was one of several pushing this rhetoric all over Silicon Valley and beyond. I was invited to give lectures, panels, and keynotes at prestigious tech conferences around the country. I was invited to give a commencement address at the Harvard Graduate School of Education. I spoke at South by Southwest. Richard Branson invited me to speak on his private island. Most of the time, I got rousing applause—sometimes even standing ovations. After every speech, my inbox was filled with notes from well-wishers (male and female) and young women who were signing on to this plan for their future. Girls Who Code grew rapidly. The takeover was in sight.

But even in those early years, something strange kept me up at night.

Every day, my staff and I interacted with dozens of young talented women who appeared ready to take on the world. In private conversation or in emails, they'd tell me that they wanted to use tech for good. They wanted to make good money and balance careers with family life. But somehow, many of these women never actually made it into tech. And those who did, didn't seem to last long. The mentorship and leadership programs we put in place helped up to a point but somehow couldn't slow their rapid exit from the field. Why?

I was also bewildered by something I discovered about many of the older women who remained in the tech sector:

There weren't any. These were the people I originally sought out to act as fund-raisers, ambassadors, and guides. But as I made my calls and wrote my emails, I could find vanishingly few who actually made it to the C-suites. The few who did were not exactly the picture of holistic wellness and contentment that our young recruits hoped to unlock with promotions and prominence at work. These older, more successful sisters were either single or divorced. Most had no children. Those who did seemed exhausted by the balance of the two or—more often—they downplayed family life, acting like their kids were enrolled at some far away, full-service, year-round boarding school that they would arrange to visit for an occasional lunch on their way back from Davos.

Somewhere, there was a deeply troubling disconnect. Where were the regular working moms—the ones who were invested in both work and family life?

This was when I finally came to see the painful truth. Or, more accurately, the Big Lie.

The Big Lie comes down to one startling fact: It makes no difference how much we lean into our careers or fight for gender parity in the workplace, or whether we partner up with "one of the good ones," because *we participate in a workforce and live in a society that do not make having it all actually possible.* Yes, the gains of the feminist movement have created extraordinary opportunities for us as women. But it has come at the unintended expense of our health, our marriages, our kids, and our peace of mind. "Having it all" is actually a horrible phrase that needs to be rooted out, as does the systemically misogynistic "opportunity" it implies. Does anyone ever hold rallies for men about how they can and should have big careers *and* big lives at the same time?

We've been striving all these years for a phantom promise that evaporates like smoke the instant we try to put our arms around it. Yes, we can have big jobs. Yes, we can have families. But no, we cannot have both in the current paradigm that exists in this country—at least not without damaging our partnerships, our career trajectory and earnings potential, the well-being of our kids, and our own mental and physical health.

INTRODUCTION

We (I) Screwed Up

I founded and am the former CEO of Girls Who Code, the largest girls' empowerment organization in the world.

I gave a TED Talk that has been viewed more than five million times urging girls and women not to allow perfectionism to stand in the way of taking risks and going after their biggest, boldest dreams.

I wrote a best-selling book called *Brave, Not Perfect* and traveled the world evangelizing women and leadership.

In speeches to hundreds of thousands of women, I preached the Gospel of Professional Ambition that promised we would succeed if we leaned in hard enough.

I upheld the feminist credo of "having it all." Yes, we could storm the C-suites *and* raise families . . . and be fulfilled doing it! All we had to do was get out of our own way.

I rallied hard behind the ideology of feminism that proclaimed we would have equality once we achieved gender parity in the workplace and dedicated my entire professional life to equipping women with the skills, training, and vision they need to take their places in the highest echelons of power.

And I was wrong.

I was wrong because telling women that having the big life they've envisioned would come solely through the hours they put in, the workplace bravery they show, and the blood, sweat, and tears they surrender is a lie.

I was wrong because as it turns out, gender equality in the workplace is a mighty and worthy thing to strive for, but it is *only one piece of the puzzle.* We will never fully have equality nor fulfillment until we make some crucial changes in our home lives, our workplaces, our culture, and in our public policies so that *all* of women's work is valued equally—both in the workplace and on the home front.

It didn't matter if I got my career "set" before starting a family. It didn't even matter if I got right to the very top, which, as the CEO of a global enterprise and best-selling author, on paper it looks like I did. Once I became the mother of two young boys, all that equality and advancement I'd fought for in the workplace did not make me exempt from also being, by societal default, the primary caretaker.

My husband, Nihal, is a good partner, but like every woman

I know, I am the home life CEO. I am the coordinator of parent-teacher conferences, birthday parties, dental checkups, sneaker replacements, flu shots, haircuts, and karate classes for my kids. I am the designated homework helper, splinter remover, weird rash identifier, lost stuffed animal finder, and itchy tag remover. I am the family event planner, transportation controller, in-house chef, social secretary, food and supplies monitor, travel agent, and both headhunter and human resources for babysitters, dog walkers, cleaners, and repairpersons. I am also the go-to when my aging parents need medical assistance or when my niece Maya needs the rental agreement for her apartment renewed. While my husband and I both run busy business enterprises by day, I also run another enterprise 24/7—the family enterprise.

And, like millions of working women like myself, I am *exhausted.*

But more than that, I'm angry.

Because beneath the glossy, shimmering feminist promise of "having it all" is a dark truth that no one told me and that I unwittingly omitted from my *rah rah* empowerment rhetoric: "Having it all" is really just a euphemism for "doing it all."

Despite the fact that the work women do at home is the backbone of our families and our economy, our society puts little to no value on it. If you ever doubt whether the work of moms is diminished, just ask full-time mothers. "Tell a person at a barbeque that you are a stay-at-home and they literally look right through you," a friend of my sister's confided in me. "It's like putting a sign on your back that says, 'I couldn't possibly have a single important or even interesting thing to say to you.' It's so sexist and so frustrating." As Aneesa Bodiat wrote in her viral *New York Times* op-ed, "No, I'm Not 'Just' a Stay-at-Home Mom," "Nobody cares how many A's I earned in high school (straight A's, in case you were wondering). Nobody cares how many degrees I have (two, both cum laude). . . . What they see, instead, are my unwashed dishes, my mediocre attempt at dinner and my kid's grubby fingernails."

Despite the fact that pre-pandemic, women comprised fifty-one percent of the labor force in America, the modern-day workforce is built around and for men. That reality is compounded for the thirty-five million working mothers in this country, as workplaces demand we leave half of our identities at home, lest we have our dedication or gravitas called into question. We are forced to exist in a workforce that tacitly stipulates we can only succeed if we act like men, and we went along with it for fear of betraying the feminist credo. Many of us act like we are okay with minimizing the impact of motherhood on our lives, pretending we are at a professional breakfast rather than parent story hour at kindergarten or apologizing profusely when an emergency call from the school nurse disrupts an all-hands meeting. But deep down, we get a sick feeling we are colluding with our own erasure. We are squeezed (or do we squeeze ourselves?) into a guilt- and shame-filled cone of silence surrounding the contradictory demands of child-rearing and professional ambition because, after all, wasn't "having it all" what we asked for? Wasn't that the dream?

That dream for working women in America has turned out to be more like a nightmare.

For years, women have been juggling the needs of our family members and our jobs, trying to live the life we had been taught to expect. We bought hook, line, and sinker into the promise of "having it all." We leaned in and aspired to the sexy, empowered #Girlboss status, but we were always straining, stressing, obsessing, worrying, trying like hell to make it all work. Book after book, article after article—some admittedly written by yours truly—offered advice and insights on how to strike a healthy work-life balance. *Delegate! Color-code your calendar to stay organized! Declare the weekends an email-free zone! Exercise!* All of which sounded lovely in theory but laughable to our overtaxed brains and cracking psyches. We had no idea it was about to get much, much worse.

Then the 2020 pandemic hit.

Within a matter of weeks of COVID-19 reaching America's shores, working women with children or relatives requiring care began to crack. As childcare facilities shut their doors and private babysitters and healthcare aides retreated to the safety of their own home bubbles, the security net made up of friends, neighbors, grandparents, and other caregivers we relied on for dear life vanished, leaving us on our own to manage the relentless and competing needs demanding attention. A Harvard/London Business School study substantiated how the pandemic considerably and inequitably ate into women's time. Harvard assistant professor Ashley Whillans noted this would translate into twelve *additional days* of chores in 2021. No one magically invented extra hours, so these chores subsumed the leisure activities like exercise and connecting with friends that directly correlate with happiness and mental health. Remember "me time"? Yeah, neither do we.

Then came the clincher. Schools closed and we suddenly had yet another full-time de facto job: teacher. Nobody asked us. Nobody stepped up to help us. Nobody told our bosses they were required to offer us flextime to make it possible for moms to survive, and certainly nobody "forgave" the fact that we could no longer keep our motherhood discreetly tucked away. There it was, unfiltered and out in the open to anyone with a Zoom login link to see.

The resulting chaos created stunning fallout. One study reported a twenty-five percent jump in anxiety disorders; another showed that in the first year of COVID-19, women's alcohol consumption rose an astronomical forty-one percent. Burnout rates spiked alarmingly as women in the workplace who were mothers or who stepped into the role of caregiver to family members who fell ill held on to their jobs and their sanity by their fingernails. The pandemic had finally exposed the silent expectations placed on American working women, revealing them as painfully contradictory and completely impossible to meet.

The scale of the carnage across the economy for working

moms was like nothing our generation had ever seen. Within months of the initial lockdown, huge swaths of the retail, child-care, education, service, and hospitality sectors—industries dominated by women—were wiped out. According to Bureau of Labor Statistics, eighty percent of the workers who left the labor force in September 2020 were women—four times the number of men—including 324,000 Latinas and 58,000 Black women. More than one million single mothers—many of whom were already living below the poverty line—lost their jobs between February and April 2020. By February 2021, 2.5 million women had left the workforce—a data point Vice President Kamala Harris proclaimed constituted a "national emergency."

Women with stable jobs who could not sustain them along with the staggering new overlay of home responsibilities were voluntarily (so to speak) exiting the workforce in droves. Texas A&M professor of business administration and psychologist Anthony Klotz coined the phrase "The Great Resignation" back in May 2021, identifying the growing trend of departures overtaking the labor force. For many Americans, the pandemic had opened their eyes to a growing dissatisfaction with their jobs or career paths, and they left in pursuit of a more fulfilling life. For many others however—most notably women and even more so women of color—the exit was necessitated by a dearth of available or affordable childcare that would enable them to work. As *Time* magazine noted in October 2020, "Many women are leaving the workforce not because their jobs have vanished but because their support systems have."

A year in, so many women had left the workplace that women's labor force participation, which had grown steadily since the 1970s, plummeted to levels not seen since the 1980s. As of September 2021, more than two million women over the age of twenty still remained out of the workforce in order to take care of their children and families—almost twice that of men of the same age.

This is all particularly sobering considering that in December 2019, just before the pandemic hit, women held more payroll jobs than men for the first time in nearly a decade. We had been the most empowered and best-educated women in the history of the world, yet suddenly we were thrown into a soul-crushing time machine that was dragging us back forty years. Silently and without debate—almost without comment—the employment gains of the feminist movement had been wiped out.

Every conversation I had with women in every sector from tech to academia revealed the frightening depths of frustration, confusion, anger, guilt, and despair we were all feeling. Women who couldn't leave the workforce were cutting back their hours; those who couldn't cut back their hours were losing their minds.

How in the world did we get here? Or were we always here but pretending we weren't? In our historic march toward equality, how could we not have seen that the doors the feminist movement cracked open in the workplace were not opened nearly wide enough to let in and keep the eighty-six percent of

American women who were or would become mothers in their lifetimes? How had educated, empowered women like me who are active in politics, with advanced degrees and boundless ambition, been conned into *hiding half of ourselves?*

This book is our chance to say four things:

1. **ENOUGH.** Enough of operating off an embarrassingly outdated model of heteronormativity and gender roles that assumes every family has two parents, one of whom stays home or works significantly less. According to the Center for American Progress, in 1960, only twenty percent of mothers worked. Today that number is at seventy percent. The U.S. Labor Department notes that seventy-five percent of these women work full-time. Enough of workplaces that are built around men, antiquated public policies that squeeze women out of the workforce, and perpetuated biases against women with children.

2. **YOU NEED US.** As the Great Resignation rages on, America faces a serious labor shortage that will never be filled if half the population is unable to work. The workforce cannot afford to lose the innovation and diversity capital of half its members, nor can our economy—or societal fabric, for that matter—survive if the plummeting birth rates continue as a result of women having to choose between working and becoming a mother.

3. **WE NEED HELP.** To employers, to our caregiving systems, to our families: We need you to step up and *pay up—*

with resources, with tangible support, with fundamental changes in how women's work is seen and valued.

4. **WE ARE NOT GOING BACK TO A BROKEN SYSTEM.** Workplaces were rigged against women from the start because they asked us to hide half of ourselves—and do it at great cost to our mental health. The future of work must include a new workplace that actually works for women. Unless real systemic changes are made, WE. ARE. NOT. COMING. BACK.

At its heart, this book is for the millions of women who know the outdated workplace model that currently exists is no longer sustainable. It is for professional working women who leaned in and, in many cases, succeeded, yet have come to the stark and painful realization that "having it all" is a lie. It is for the women who are afraid to speak up about their home commitments for fear they won't be taken seriously in the workplace, and for the younger generation of women who are looking at a future in which they wonder if they can reasonably hold on to their ambitions *and* dreams of having a family. In this book I refer to my own heteronormative marriage, but the issues and challenges apply to all women: Black, brown, or white; straight or LGBTQ; married or single; intern or industry leader.

For all women, it will equip us with real tools to go up against the powerful forces that view motherhood as a personal and professional inconvenience instead of the foundation on which our society rests, and that dismiss our unpaid domestic labor as inconsequential rather than the essential hand that keeps the fabric of families in America from unraveling. This is a call for a revolution that needs to pick up where the feminist movement left off. My mentor and friend Hillary Clinton famously said that women's rights are human rights, and to that I add that mothers' rights are every bit as crucial.

But this book is also for the stakeholders who need us in order to survive. It is for employers—from corporate CEOs to shop owners to institutional administrators—who know they need to make systemic changes in order to retain top talent and position their companies for the new, post-pandemic reality. It is for the policymakers who decided to cut parental leave in President Joe Biden's Build Back Better bill, and yes, for the family members who also need to call for changes in their workplaces (and in their internalized biases) to give the women they rely on the respect and support they need.

This book is not a gripe about domestic partners who don't do enough, or a ten-part plan of how to fix them. It is not a litany of complaints about misogyny, society, governmental policies, or even our broken childcare system. And it most definitely is not another *rah, rah, rah* guide for women on how to score the corner office. It is a clear-eyed look at the seismic shift in our workforce that revealed the reality in which we as women and breadwinners exist, an understanding of how we as a society got here, and—most importantly—a road map for change.

It took COVID-19 to rip the bandage off the ugly, festering, long-ignored wound that so many women share: that our work and dreams are not only taken for granted but viewed as expendable. As the default caregivers, we have become the unacknowledged, unpaid safety net in our country that invisibly holds everything together, and the pressure that places on us has become intolerable. This book is a call to action to make the systemic changes in our societal power dynamics when it comes to everything from pay to gender roles to how we define and value women's domestic contributions in our culture.

This is a once-in-a-generation opportunity that *must not be missed* to redefine the future of women and work. A future in which the work of labor in the home is valued and compensated on par with the labor in paid jobs, in which quality, affordable childcare, and paid parental leave are understood as essential to preserving the innovation and diverse capital women bring to the workforce; one in which workers' wellness is valued just as much as their output and women no longer have to hide half their identities in order to succeed.

As Amanda Gorman so eloquently reminded us, silence doesn't mean peace. Women have silently suffered in this unsustainable reality for far too long, and we are not willing to remain complicit in the demise of our ambitions and sanity one more day. We cannot—no, we *will not*—support a workforce and economy that refuses to support us in return.

Let's get loud and finish this fight once and for all.

PART ONE

—

The Open Secret of Women and Work

1

Something Has to Give

Burned out. Exhausted. Depressed. Enraged.

Women are at a breaking point.

The pandemic completely upended our work, our families, our worlds. It lay waste to our ambition and our relationships; the rage and despair it wrought was palpable. But the truth is, this has been a long time coming.

According to the International Labour Organization, Americans work longer hours than any other industrialized nation in the world. With one in five of us suffering from mental health issues, we pay the price for it. Health researchers suggest women work no more than thirty-four hours per week. That sounds reasonable. Yet sixty-six percent of American women surpass that, clocking in more than forty hours at their jobs on a weekly basis. And that is *before* the 5.7 hours they spend daily doing the unpaid labor of household chores and taking care of children and elders (two hours more per day than men).

The long, inflexible hours and full dedication that most jobs demand conflict directly with the work of gestating, birthing, and caring for our children and running our homes. Nearly half of all Americans in their forties and fifties with parents over age sixty-five and young children, known as the "sandwich generation," find themselves not only working these long hours but also mired in the heavy caretaking and financial needs of both. Forget about finding time for all that "self-care" we're supposed to be doing to preserve our well-being, like seeing friends, exercising, pursuing fulfilling hobbies, or even just *breathing*. Younger women say they're so busy with work that they don't have time to think about dating.

The sick, sad, lonely struggle that women have endured trying to be everything to everybody has also created a sort of generational trauma, subverting the ambitions of young women and eroding their sense of agency in their own destiny. As one twenty-eight-year-old who works in my company said, "I look around at all of you—no offense—and think there's no way I want to put myself through that." Ouch. But I understand her perspective. What's attractive about being stretched too thin, being overlooked at home and judged hard at work, or feeling like an inadequate and taken-for-granted caretaker?

No woman who is or wants to be a mother, regardless of race or socioeconomic status, is exempt from the impossible demands. However, for some, these demands are even more crushing. Twenty-four percent of mothers in the United States are single moms without a partner to fall back on. The numbers are higher for women of color; more than half of Black mothers and one-fourth of Latina mothers are raising their children on their own. According to the Brookings Institute, Black women face the toughest childcare crunch. They earn considerably less than their white counterparts, so most don't have the financial resources to step away from their jobs to care for their kids and, at the same time, cite prohibitive costs as a barrier to securing childcare. For many of those who can afford it, it doesn't matter anyway because they live in "childcare deserts" where options are scarce.

I am keenly aware that I am speaking from a privileged, heteronormative vantage point—and that my struggles are nominal compared to women who worry from day to day about feeding their families let alone managing all their opposing responsibilities. Yet that does not negate the realities of a jerry-rigged system that is not working for any of us. Those with the means turn to a roster of babysitters, tutors, and house cleaners to help raise our kids and keep our home lives afloat while we work. Many of these women end up barely breaking even, begging the question men are almost never forced to ask themselves: Can I afford to work? For the four out of ten families in which women are the primary breadwinners, this isn't a question they have the luxury to ponder.

In turn, the caregivers who are hired to care for other women's children—many of whom come from marginalized communities—are forced to create a patchwork of coping strategies to meet the needs of their own children and families. Like millions of working mothers who struggle to make ends meet, they turn to friends, relatives, and community-run afterschool programs for help and relief.

Many of the older feminist activists I have spoken to say they thought society would move faster than it has, that equality was just around the corner. They believed that the division of labor at work and home would evolve as barriers to education, training, and jobs fell away. But the grim facts are clear: No matter how much women earn, where they live, or what political party they vote for, they still end up doing about twice as much housework and child-rearing as their male partners. And although it's killing us, we're supposed to act like that's okay.

The story of domestic inequality and working women's struggles isn't new; this reality has been hiding in plain sight for years. What is new, however, is that when the pandemic washed away all the tenuous arrangements of work-life balance we'd all cobbled together, it also washed away the pretense that the system as it currently exists is even remotely sustainable. Our reality was finally out there, raw and exposed in broad daylight for all to see.

This is not working for anyone. All of us—generationally, racially, socioeconomically—find our tether to our work and wages grow more precarious even as we fight to smash glass ceilings. All of us, no matter what neighborhood we live in or what jobs we do, grapple with the realization that we are trying and constantly failing to catch up.

Something has to give.

MY MELTDOWN MOMENT

I was lying in the fetal position on the rug in my son's bedroom at 5 p.m. on a gray Tuesday, a blue Lego knifing into my left cheek. We were deep into the winter days of the pandemic, and I was overwhelmed and tired, not just in my mind and body, but deep in my soul. I felt so heavy. Every ounce of my being was depleted, weary, and—in a word—done.

I am one of the lucky ones. I know this. I am gainfully employed. I have a husband I love, two healthy boys, and the resources to hire help. Who was I to complain when people all over the world were losing their jobs and, worse, their beloved family members to this dreaded virus? What right did I have to feel like the bottom was falling out of my universe?

And yet, there I was, pinned to the carpet by a heavy black hopelessness that felt palpable. It wasn't until much later that I would come to understand that I had joined the ranks of the more than two million working women in America who were suffering from extreme burnout since the start of the pandemic and the countless more who were reaching their breaking point under the strain of deadly virus fears, school closures, full-time work (which may or may not disappear from under us), a maddening discrepancy in household duties and lack of support, and the loss of our ambition, dreams, and sense of self as we knew it.

Still desperate to cling to my identity as a girlboss, I was wearing my "work from home" uniform: conservative earrings, a pressed blouse, dirty pajama bottoms, and bunched gray socks. My day had started twelve hours earlier at 5:30 a.m. with five-month-old baby Sai screaming in his crib. Having collapsed into bed only six hours earlier after finishing Girls Who Code's emergency strategic plan, I hauled myself out of bed with only a passing envious glance at my husband, Nihal, still snoring softly. I shuffled down the hall to rescue Sai from his diaper that was soaked through and reeking. I cleaned him up, hoisted him onto my right hip, and headed to the kitchen to make breakfast for him and our older son, Shaan, then five.

Next came the daily morning battle. Schools were closed, so Shaan's education was taking place at the dining room table, which, like nearly every mom of young kids in America, meant I was the de facto morning bell, teaching assistant, tech support, and guidance counselor all rolled into one. Luring him away from the television, out of his pajamas, and in front of the Zoom camera for laptop kindergarten took the patience and tact of a hostage negotiator. By 8:15 a.m. when he was finally logged on, I was exhausted. When Nihal rolled into the kitchen at 8:30 a.m., I handed him the baby and made a beeline for the desk shoved against the wall in our bedroom that served as my new office.

I threw off my pajama top, which smelled like a wet diaper,

and put on the nearest (frankly, not terribly fresh) blouse to appear halfway presentable for my 8:45 a.m. meeting. My blood pressure dropped slightly when I heard our babysitter, Audrey, open the apartment door. For probably the thousandth time, my mind went to the millions of women who didn't have a lifeline like Audrey showing up. I grew up as a latchkey kid of two working parents who could not afford a babysitter, so I appreciate how extraordinarily privileged I am as a parent to have the resources to secure help in any capacity at all. While the benefit of that luxury was never lost on me, it took on entirely new depths during lockdown.

Within minutes I was immersed in an emergency Zoom session with my colleagues, trying to figure out how we could shore up our organization which, like so many others around the country, was suddenly struggling to survive. Just as we got into a flow of engaged and thoughtful brainstorming, Shaan began kicking the door of my "office" demanding a chocolate chip muffin. By midday, I'd missed an important meeting with a promising funder because the baby woke up just as Shaan's lunch period began. Late afternoon I received a regretful resignation of a key staff member and mother of two who explained she couldn't handle balancing her work and home life, followed by an email from my sister asking for help finding an assisted living facility for an aging family friend.

Now the day was ending. Audrey had gone home and I was due to officially clock in for what sociologist Arlie Hochschild had aptly labeled "the second shift"—the work we do at home after our paid day's labor had ended. Dinner prep, a pile of ripe laundry, a sink full of dishes, and the bedtime tug-of-war with Shaan were waiting for me to get up off that rug.

Nihal opened the door and I felt, rather than saw, a shaft of light from the hallway illuminate my form on the floor. In years past, I would have told you that I love my husband tenderly. But lately, it seemed I carried a dark cloud of resentment into every interaction we had. During COVID, we fought almost constantly.

"Where's Mommy?" I heard Shaan inquire.

"Mommy's taking a nap," Nihal responded softly.

"Mommy never takes a nap," replied Shaan, sounding doubtful.

The door closed and their conversation continued as they disappeared down the hall, their words growing indistinct. I felt like my limbs were made of lead and wondered if I could lie there on my son's rug forever.

But of course, I couldn't, and I didn't. I robotically made dinner—nothing you'd post on Instagram but reasonably nutritious. Without thinking too much, I did the dishes and threw in a full load of laundry. Somewhere beneath my right eyebrow, a headache was forming. Determined to block out the chaos that threatened to overwhelm the rest of the apartment, I ran the children through their bath, book, and bedtime routine, then sat down for a few hours to hack through the work I hadn't gotten to since the morning. As I walked past Nihal asleep on the sectional cradling the remote, he stirred and, likely seeing my exhaustion, mumbled using his affection-ate term for me, "Munch, you okay?"

Not trusting myself to speak (or not to rip into him like a she-bitch from hell), I nodded silently and continued on to our bedroom, where I popped a 5 mg CBD gummy that did little to allay the rising panic as I thought about how the chaos would begin all over again tomorrow.

No, Munch wasn't okay. Far from it.

THE MOTHERHOOD MYTH

As I usually do in moments like these, I called my best friend, Deepa. Deepa is a professor of legal studies at Georgia State University's College of Business and the mom of two grade-school kids. After some generic complaining about going stir-crazy, wiping down groceries, and the hour-after-hour scheduled Zoom calls to field work crises, I told her about my experience lying on Shaan's floor. Two weeks ago, she said, something similar had happened to her.

"I was in the middle of doing a hundred different things, multitasking like a lunatic," she said. "And then, suddenly, noth-ing. I literally could not stand up out of my chair. It was like my battery died."

What was happening to us, we wondered. But we knew. We knew. All the months and years of juggling, all the stressing, all the precisely calibrated schedules and systems we put in place that blew apart with shocking ease at the slightest hiccup

(*Arghh, babysitter can't come because there's a snowstorm . . .*), the onslaught of daily tasks that added up to what felt like death by a thousand details. We'd been skating on the proverbial thin ice for so long that when we finally crashed through to the icy waters below, we had no strength or wherewithal left to swim to safety.

For years, like Deepa and so many other women, I, too, had been going a hundred miles an hour, all day every day, multitasking so incessantly that I thought I'd go crazy. My mind was never fully on one thing, and everything and everyone suffered for it, me included. I was always running late, rescheduling meetings if I even remembered I had them at all. I stood on the playground with my cell phone pressed against my ear, coaching someone on my staff about how to salvage an important funding relationship that was falling apart while from the top of the slide Shaan clamored over and over, "Watch me, Mommy! Watch me!" We'd go out to dinner with friends in an attempt to be social adults, but I'd spend the entire time texting the babysitter. *Is Shaan still awake? Did the rash on his back look any better?* This would annoy Nihal and then we'd fight the whole way home. I'd put Shaan to bed every night only to have him pop up minutes later, screeching that he was scared of the dark and begging me to stay in his room for hours, night after night. I'd sit there in the dark knowing I should feel good that I was comforting my son but instead feeling sickeningly guilty because I actually *just wanted to escape.*

I didn't think motherhood would be like this. With a full

heart and unswerving enthusiasm, I had committed to do the most important job in America: having kids and raising them to become the upstanding citizens and capable, intelligent, adaptable workers of tomorrow. Wasn't it supposed to feel . . . *wonderful?* Or at the very least, not horrible?

From the time I was a little girl, I craved having a family and being a mom. I met and married Nihal in 2012, then a part-time DJ who had just recently launched a popular start-up, and very soon after we set out to start a family.

For all my excitement about conceiving and my public speeches about women's empowerment, I was stunned to find out becoming a mom wasn't empowering at all—just exhausting. I was physically depleted, psychologically fragmented. I proudly took only a month off then I was back online, running my organization, raising money, traveling, and speaking. I even brought Shaan with me to some speaking engagements to prove (to myself, maybe?) that a baby would not slow me down.

But the reality was that I was faltering. I tried—oh my God, how I tried to keep up at work, and I'm lucky to have had a stellar team that could not have been more supportive. Despite having a babysitter to be with Shaan during the workday, I could feel myself slipping—losing sight of all the things I wanted for myself. I could reel off the garbage bag size for the kitchen waste basket (13 gallons), the growth rate of Shaan's pudgy little feet (Q: new shoes already? A: yes), and the use-by date on the milk in the fridge, but I couldn't tell you the last time I'd read a full article in the newspaper.

The maddening part was that each task on my to-do list, taken on its own, was inconsequential and completely trivial. But in the aggregate, they were essential. If the tasks weren't accomplished, my home life would suffer and it would negatively impact someone I loved very deeply—my husband, our infant son, or my aging relatives.

And then there was Shaan, the light of our lives. He was an easygoing infant but once he became a toddler, it became clear he was a little human all his own with needs, wants, and moods, few of which would occur on a predictable schedule or neatly accommodate his parents' adult wishes or rhythms. Starting a family was supposed to be the highlight of my life, but somehow, motherhood was not the enriching experience I imagined could be easily integrated into my life. Taking a baby to the Women's March in Washington, D.C., where you're scheduled to speak sounds like a badass idea until said baby throws up all over your jacket moments before you take the mic in front of millions and refuses to stop crying when you are about to go on, so you decide to just take him with you onstage and pray.

Motherhood, as it turned out, was making my work life unbearable—and vice versa.

WHAT HAPPENED TO MY LIFE?

I'm embarrassed to tell you that amid all this intolerable guilt and stress during Shaan's early years, I turned on my husband, whom I love very much, with a fury.

Nihal's company offered twelve weeks of paid paternity leave and while no one encouraged him to take it, he stayed home for a few weeks while Shaan and I "got settled" and then headed back to work. Every morning when he walked out the door, I swallowed back bitter words, jealous of his freedom. Everything was still normal for him, but I was now the CEO of both my company and our family unit.

Nihal had his hands full at work and when he was home, he was tired and distracted. He was constantly on his phone working and it was killing me. His long hours and circadian rhythm made it difficult for him to wake up early in the morning, so I usually took the first watch, making breakfast, changing Shaan into his clothes and running the laundry, and taking him to school while doing a call on the way.

I would ask Nihal for help and he would say, "I never played with dolls, so I don't know how to do it."

"I never played with cars, but I know how to drive!" I'd shout back.

I felt humiliated and abandoned. We fought almost constantly. My resentments made me unrecognizable to my husband—and to myself.

I'd tell him he needed to do more. He'd say he was doing more, but he also needed to show up for work. I'd say I have to show up for work. He'd say he'd try. But inevitably, I was the one interacting with the pediatrician about Shaan's earache and staying up late at night poring over the current medical thinking on Eustachian tubes or arranging overnight childcare so we could attend a friend's wedding. It was absurd. What qualified me any more than him to decide about ear surgery for the baby? Nihal didn't even read the articles I sent him from PubMed. There was a way in which we would simply not engage and I swear, it felt strategic. He didn't do it, so I had to. The United States is the country with the largest drop in marital happiness following the birth of a child.

Despite our high levels of conflict, in 2018 Nihal and I decided to have a second child. Just as we brought home our beautiful newborn son, Sai, in 2020, the world began shutting down. My company's future was thrown into question, so I immediately ended my maternity leave even though Sai was just a few weeks old. My rosy plans for a relaxing maternity leave during which I could celebrate the end of a decade of fertility struggles, unplug from work, and reset my relationship with my husband and now five-year-old Shaan, quickly evaporated.

At first, I tried to maintain a healthy balance between being there for my family, my coworkers, and myself. I'd wake up early with the baby, try to muster the energy for a quick workout, and then immediately hop on a war room call with my senior leadership team. But as the days passed, I started losing pieces of my health and my mind. Eventually I could just barely drag myself to the computer screen and stare listlessly at the square tiles containing the exhausted faces of my female colleagues who were now also living their own private hells.

It was sometime around mid-October when the unending demands from both work and family finally started to pull me under. I was being yanked in three directions at once, all day every day. During a work call, my colleagues could hear Shaan shouting as he played ninja pirate with his friend Wally on FaceTime, the baby crying in the background, and Nihal asking me if I bought bananas. I was gaining weight and eating too much sugar, which is especially not good because I am pre-diabetic. My face broke out in acne that I hadn't seen since I was sixteen. I had raging insomnia. I later learned that I'd contracted COVID. My symptoms were mild, thank goodness, so I barely let it register. I didn't have the time.

Slowly, and then suddenly with the pandemic, it had all become too much.

OUR COLLECTIVE PRIMAL SCREAM

As the days turned into weeks, I began to notice that my experience was far from an anomaly—in fact, it seemed to be the norm. News outlets ran story after story about burned-out women and struggling moms, as women were flaming out at a rate unlike anything the world had ever seen. Nearly a third of the thirty-five million working moms in America in late 2020 were suffering from symptoms of burnout, which include headaches, chest tightness, fatigue, hair loss, nausea, lack of motivation, irritability, cynicism, and increased crying. More than half the mothers with children under the age of eighteen reported a marked decrease in their mental health since COVID-19 began.

As Helen Lewis wrote in her article in *The Atlantic*, "The Pandemic Has Given Women a New Kind of Rage," women were more than just sad. They were more than burned out. They were *furious*. Furious that bars stayed open but schools closed. Furious about the disproportionate job losses women were facing, especially women of color. Furious about the inequity at home that was making work impossible and bosses who told them they needed to stop mentioning their children as an "excuse" not to work.

Some turned the rage on themselves. Back in 1963, Betty Friedan reported in her groundbreaking work, *The Feminine Mystique*, that to cope with the pressure from the roles placed on them by society, women were "taking tranquilizers like cough drops." In 2020, the proverbial "mother's little helper" seemed to come more often out of a wine cellar than a pill bottle. In our pre-pandemic life, posts about Mommy day-drinking (vodka in the water bottle at soccer games, wine spritzers at playdates), boozy book groups, "Rosé All Day" T-shirts, and lighthearted memes had been a Mommy Blog staple. The gaiety belied the dangerous truth that women's drinking had been on the rise for two decades. The National Institute on Alcohol Abuse and Alcoholism reports that women of all ages are drinking more than they did a decade ago, and that alcohol use disorder in women more than doubled between 2000 and 2016. As mothers with children under the age of five increased their drinking by a staggering 323 percent in the days since COVID and beyond, no one's laughing about "Mommy Juice" anymore.

Then came the conversation that started to turn things around for me. As I continued to share the stories I had been hearing and reading, my friend Madhu remarked, "We've been mired in this muck for a long, long time. Something has to change. No . . . I take that back. *Everything* has to change." Then she issued the challenge that pinged around my head for days: "You're the activist here, Resh. How do we change this?"

WE HAD IT ALL WRONG

That night, as I walked around and around my apartment with Sai on my shoulder to soothe him in the wee hours, I began to think about the whole idea of women's empowerment. Did we get it all wrong? For so many years, I'd been preaching the Gospel of Professional Ambition that had been so warmly embraced by the feminist movement and corporate America. I went over and over the Gospel in my head.

The first part: If we leaned in enough and worked hard enough, we'd get ahead and make strides toward equality in the workplace.

Okay: check.

We did lean in. We did fight like hell and while we're not there yet, we made huge strides over the past forty years breaking the glass ceiling. Forty-one women now hold the top spots at Fortune 500 companies. Close to twenty percent of VC funding in 2021 went to start-ups led by women. A record number of women serve in Congress as of 2021, up fifty percent from ten years ago. We have a woman vice president, for goodness' sake.

The second part: And when we achieved equality in the workplace, we'd be happy.

Oops.

It was then that I realized we needed a new gospel. No— scratch that. We didn't need any more gospel from above. We needed a boots-on-the-ground plan.

No more trumpeting that women's tenacity alone will change this—that by stampeding into the workforce, our sheer numbers and hard work will allow us to achieve equality. We need the *system* to change. We will never achieve the kind of equality we were raised to expect and that the twentieth century feminists fought so hard for until we change some fundamental things about our workplaces, our home life, our culture, and our governmental support.

We needed a plan.

One in four mothers go back to work less than two weeks after giving birth. If we leave for even just a year to take care of our children, elderly parents, or manage an illness of our own, we would lose about forty percent of our income. It was time to call out these policies for what they were—institutionalized misogyny. And it needed to end.

I began to feel a great wellspring of energy around speaking the truth about what motherhood really looks like and what the future of work needed to be for women across America. One after the other, the words to define our reality and our needs started becoming clear.

Women in the workforce should not have to pay a penalty for having children. We cannot and should not have to hide, minimize, and multitask while awkwardly and apologetically wedging our motherhood or other caretaking responsibilities into the scant hours between work and sleep.

Women are no less dedicated to their jobs just because they have children. All things being equal, I'd hire a mom ten times over because we're the ones who know how to juggle a million things at once, which is in fact the ideal worker. You say distracted? I say *equipped*.

We don't need to break more glass ceilings. We don't need more mentorship. We don't need more conferences about women's empowerment in the workplace. We need a workplace that is not designed around men.

We need to get off the proverbial seesaw we've been riding for far too long: the one on which the equally weighty but naturally opposing forces of paid labor at work and invisible labor at home compete for leverage. Balance is, of course, an illusion. One side is always up while the other is down, the latter more often than not smacking to the ground with a resounding thud.

We don't need more self-help advice on how to ride the ups and downs. We don't need more tools to fix the seesaw when it breaks down.

We needed a plan to dismantle the damn seesaw and get on a whole new ride.

We must take apart everything we know and assume about women and work and put the pieces back together in a completely reimagined configuration. According to a study conducted in the spring of 2020 by the *New York Times*, seventy percent of working women say they handle the majority of childcare. We need to either reset the equation or make this visible and valued. Or better yet, both.

Women cannot do it all. We cannot work to our highest potential *and* raise our kids *and* be the CEO of our families' lives *and* manage our households. That is, not without real, tangible support. Not without acknowledgment of the unpaid, invisible work we do to raise this country's next generations. Not without the recognition that motherhood is a job that deserves as much respect and compensation as the corner office, and that caring for children and running a family enterprise is a mission that is critical for the future of our community, our economy, and our country. More than that, we shouldn't have to.

The pandemic decimated women's careers and forced a staggering twelve million women from the workforce, but the return to office presents the single biggest opportunity we have seen in modern times to reboot our workplace.

So, what now? How would we stem the bleeding and bring them back since, as economist Luke Pardue and others have pointed out, we will never fully recover from the economic crisis rendered by the pandemic until we get women back into the workforce in rates equal to men? What was the strategy to end women being forced to choose between populating the world and earning a living? Where were the leaders and the legislators to institute new policies, the forward-thinking employers to transform the workplace, the culture disruptors and sociological experts to help make motherhood desirable again? How could we seize this once-in-a-generation opportunity to change the future and meaning of work as we know it?

We needed a plan, dammit.

2

The Marshall Plan for Moms

How could we mobilize the current administration, employers, and the culture at large to make the big changes we needed? What would a plan look like to radically reshape the future of work so that it was no longer rigged against working mothers? What were the mechanisms we needed to put in place to get our workplaces and our government to *pay up* for the unseen, unpaid labor of mothers—via respect, recognition, and actual cold, hard cash?

The only parallel I could think of was the Marshall Plan established by the United States after World War II to help salvage Western Europe. The war had leveled entire cities and towns, decimated national economies, caused a staggering seventy to eight-five million deaths, and badly damaged the psyches and lives of millions of survivors. Of course, I'm not equating the effect of the pandemic on moms with the millions of war dead or the sickening atrocities of the Holo-caust. It was the recovery plan that I was sourcing as inspira-tion. Back then, our political leaders saw the photographs of the landscapes reduced to rubble and knew without question that lives had been seismically upended and that the bonds of families, work, community, and country had been stressed to the breaking point. They also knew that a comprehensive, 360-degree plan to rebuild was critical for the world to heal and European economies to find new and stable footing. In the wake of the pandemic, the bonds of family and sustain-ability of work were also badly damaged. In many cases, the plans for economic stability that the feminist movement had fought so hard for went up in smoke. Yet where were the lead-ers stepping in to help rebuild the scorched earth beneath our feet?

What resulted was an op-ed I banged out calling for a Mar-shall Plan for Moms. I wrote what was obvious to me and so many others: that moms, and especially wage-earning moms, were getting crushed and that the ambition and work capital of half an entire generation were being erased. I called for a comprehensive, point-by-point plan of economic and societal recovery for mothers. I argued that in order to realize this re-covery, we needed to win some basic support for moms: pay equity, paid sick leave, and affordable childcare—things that were long overdue. I called for direct payments to moms, who in the pandemic had seen their paid labor in the workforce supplanted by unpaid labor at home. I laid out the raw truth:

that COVID and the mass exodus of women from the work-force it caused proved once and for all that America needed to step up and fundamentally change how it valued and supported mothers.

For the most part, these ideas were not new—groups like the National Domestic Workers Alliance, Paid Leave for All, Oxfam, and the National Women's Law Center had been pushing for them to be codified into law for decades. But Congress would not give them any oxygen.

I sent it to the editor of *The Hill*, which had featured the work of my nonprofit in the past. To my surprise, he posted it without much comment. I was happy to see before I went to bed that more than several dozen people had read it. By the time I woke up the next morning, it had gone from a few dozen to a few thousand and was going viral, popping up repeatedly in reposts on my feed on Facebook, Twitter, and Instagram. My cell phone was blowing up with calls from friends, old colleagues, moms I knew from Shaan's school saying, as one mom put it, "I cried when I read your piece; I felt for the first time that someone finally saw me." I went from feeling isolated and trapped in a bubble of anger and despair to realizing that I was far from alone in my belief that moms deserved support. Maybe, just maybe the Marshall Plan for Moms should be more than just an angry op-ed.

I'd always thought activism was about fixing problems *out there*, for others. Turned out that my personal struggles as a working mom weren't just personal, but a societal wrong that

needed an overhaul. It wasn't just me stomping my feet saying that companies and government should step up to support
us in our contradictory roles as contributing members to the
workforce and as mothers. What does it say about our culture
that I am one of the privileged women with a stable partner, a
solid career, and the financial resources to hire help and run
my household—and yet I am *still* drowning under the conflict-
ing demands of work and raising children?

It was quickly becoming clear that on a massive scale, the
center could no longer hold. Working motherhood in America
was broken and we needed collective action to fix it.

AMPLIFYING THE PRIMAL SCREAM

I knew that if we wanted to really achieve the big systemic
changes mothers needed and deserved, we'd need to take our
fight straight to the top.

I've been a political activist in one form or another since I
was in my late twenties, when I left a high-paying job as a corporate lawyer to follow my dream of running for Congress. Although my race garnered national attention (*South Asian young
upstart takes on the political establishment!*) I lost, but it galvanized
me to fight even harder for the rights of girls and women by
leveling the playing field for them in the high-powered tech
sector. With the white-hot passion of activism running through
my veins once again, I knew what we needed to do next. We
needed to capture the attention of corporate CEOs, lawmak-

ers, and most essentially, the president of the United States. The way: a full-page ad in the *New York Times*.

I pulled together a coalition of prominent business leaders, activists, and celebrities to sign with me a full-page ad in the *New York Times* calling for a Marshall Plan for Moms. The list included Charlize Theron, Amy Schumer, Eva Longoria, Julianne Moore, and Gabrielle Union, along with Alexis McGill Johnson, president and CEO of Planned Parenthood; Tarana Burke, founder of the #metoo movement; Maria Teresa Kumar, founder and CEO of Voto Latino; and the founders of ClassPass, SHE Summit, Birchbox, The Cru, and Rent the Runway. The plan called on President Biden to create a task force to institute a Marshall Plan for Moms and implement a direct payment to moms within the first one hundred days of his administration. Our demands, tone, and purpose were direct and clear:

"Sound crazy? It's not. It's time to put a dollar figure on our labor. Motherhood isn't a favor and it's not a luxury. It's a job. The first 100 days are an opportunity to define our values. So let's start by valuing moms."

By the next morning, the primal scream of moms became the 2020 feminist shot heard 'round the world.

Within twenty-four hours, news outlets from across the globe were calling me for interviews and I was thrust onto center stage under a hot spotlight. Needless to say, with my gray roots and pallor courtesy of eight months trapped at home and fried working-mom-during-the-pandemic brain, I was unprepared.

The very first thing I did was drag lights into the corner of my bedroom so I could do Zoom interviews without the background sounds of my kids screaming. The irony of this was not lost on me. Here I was, on the international stage calling for a radical reinvention of the workplace so working mothers no longer had to hide their motherhood in order to succeed, and I was still personally trapped under the heavy boulder of societal expectations (Note to self: in addition to changes in the workplace, family dynamics, and governmental policies, we needed to change a few fundamental things about how we as working mothers show up, too).

Then I called my senior leadership team to bounce talking points off them. I needed to get my brain working again. Within days, I became a go-to guest on every major broadcast outlet from *Good Morning America* to *CBS Evening News with Norah O'Donnell*. Articles about the Marshall Plan for Moms appeared in hundreds of publications online and in print all across the United States and even in the United Kingdom. Even articles that did not directly reference the Marshall Plan for Moms articulated the primal scream of mothers nationwide. Within weeks, we had gotten more than one billion impressions on social media. The message was resonating far and wide.

We quickly followed up with a letter of support published in the *Washington Post* signed by fifty prominent men including athletes Steph Curry and Victor Cruz, actors Don Cheadle and Colin Farrell, craigslist founder Craig Newmark, Reddit co-founder Alexis Ohanian, and Care.com CEO Tim Allen. The letter emphasized the pressing need for economic relief and systemic change—including within family dynamics:

"When more than 30 years of progress for women in the workforce can be erased in 9 months, the underlying system is broken. It's time to create a new structure that works for women, that respects and values their labor," the letter reads. "Men have a role to play. As partners and fathers we need to start doing our share at home. Studies show we are failing."

The movement garnered not only attention as a result of these ads but real traction. Lawmakers in both the House and Senate including Congresswoman Grace Meng and Senator Amy Klobuchar introduced resolutions in support of the Marshall Plan for Moms. A handful of states have introduced bills. New York City and Los Angeles have convened task forces. Turning up the volume on this issue helped shape the narrative around expansion of the child tax credit and many of the policies headlining President Biden's American Families Plan. But even with all that, the fight is far from over. In fact, this November as Congress was negotiating the Build Back Better

Plan, the first policy that was put on the chopping block was paid leave. This, even though the United States is the only developed nation that doesn't offer paid leave. This, despite the fact that Democrats control both the White House and Congress and we may never have this opportunity again for a very long time. This, even when women are being pushed from the labor force because basic supports like paid leave are not available to them and are begging for help from the government. Still the first thing they decide to let go and negotiate out: paid leave.

The saddest part is that women were not the least bit surprised.

THE FUTURE OF WORK

Over the course of the past two decades, corporate feminism has savvily sold us a pop version of feminist progress, packaged in pink pussy hats, Notorious RBG swag, glossy pictures of women on corporate homepages, and gauzy campaigns to support Women's History Month. But don't be fooled. We had all that and the workplace still didn't work for women.

More public relations campaigns aren't going to get us there. Instagram pictures showing a baby shower for a pregnant employee hosted in the breakroom aren't going to get us there. What's needed to change the future of work for women runs much deeper than good intentions and surface optics.

When a top manager signals, however indirectly, that a

woman's pregnancy and motherhood responsibilities are a "burden" on other staffers because she needs to pause a meeting to answer a text from her kid, or that being "off duty" (and off email) in the evenings and on weekends makes you a less than ideal employee, that a staff meeting is more important than picking up a sick child from school, or when she is materially underpaid on her parental leave by a multibillion-dollar company—Amazon—and has to write Jeff Bezos directly to fix the mistake so she can pay her bills, we need to call this out for what it is: corrosive practices that drive women from the workforce.

We need to rethink the outdated economic models that have erased the impact of the essential work traditionally done by women. We need to reexamine some of the widely accepted messages of the American feminist movement. We need to create workplaces that are not built around only men. We need to start talking about and to corporate leaders, managers, workers, political leaders, and policymakers who need to radically redefine the workplace so it works for women.

And we need to do it *now*.

Why the urgency? First and foremost, as you already saw, COVID-19 ushered in an alarming mental health crisis for women as they were squeezed out of the workforce. Numerous studies show that women and girls were disproportionately hit during the pandemic. Women across thirty-eight countries experienced a threefold increase in mental health struggles compared to men, and reports of post-traumatic stress disorder, anxiety, and depression skyrocketed. Philip Fisher, a professor of psychology at the University of Oregon who has conducted numerous national surveys on the impact of the pandemic on parents of young children, speaks to how mothers in particular were affected more drastically because of the many intersectional challenges they face, including economic constraints, being single breadwinners, or caring for children with special needs.

As we inch our way out of what was hopefully the worst of the pandemic, a new working model that promises "flexibility" has arisen, yet this new paradigm threatens to further derail the mental health of working mothers, demanding they are now on 24/7 in both parenting *and* work roles. As an article on the tech news website *Recode* noted, working from home for women is vastly different than it is for men thanks to deeply ingrained inequalities in expected gender roles. A crying toddler, for instance, is far more likely to interrupt a woman's Zoom call, and a woman is more likely to pause her day to do domestic chores to keep the household running. It's no wonder McKinsey cited a gross disparity in 2020 between the satisfaction of women and men working remotely; seventy-nine percent of men reported having a positive experience working from home compared to thirty-seven percent of women.

This is not the first time that a "liberating" trend sold to women backfired. Back in the 1950s, appliance companies ran cheery ads extolling the freedom that all the new-fangled cooking appliances, dishwashers, and washing machines would afford housewives. Before, they could only cook dinner . . . but now they can do it *while doing the laundry*! The innovations that promised to free up their energy and time only did so to enable them to multitask more housework. If we do not redefine work in this new paradigm before it becomes ingrained as the new norm, the crisis for women's mental health will go as unchecked as the "liberating" housework piled on our plates.

Without making deep systemic changes, we risk the mass exodus of women leaving the workforce during the pandemic being only the tip of the economic iceberg. In the month of September 2021 alone, 865,000 exited the workforce. As Rachel Thomas, CEO of Lean In remarked at the time, "If we had a panic button, we'd be hitting it. We have never seen numbers like these." Imagine if the labor force continued to bleed out at that rate. The industries that employ mostly women, including education, childcare, healthcare, domestic service, restaurants, and retail will be more than just crippled. They will be decimated. The vicious cycle will then grow wider and deeper as the dearth of childcare options forces even more working mothers to leave their jobs. For the forty percent of American women for whom working is a necessity for survival, this is no joke. On a broader scale, this may go without saying, but picturing a world in which women no longer have enough income to be economically independent is pretty scary.

Imagine if the plummeting birthrate in this country— which in 2020 hit its lowest point in fifty years—continued to decline as younger women eyeball the dueling demands of career and motherhood and say an emphatic "no thank you." Experts are already noting that this trend suggests the current generation will not be able to replace themselves without immigration. We will face economic challenges resulting from fewer people paying into Social Security; a shortage of workers to fill essential jobs will damage productivity and threaten our position as a world economic leader. In that light, the dystopian fiction of *The Handmaid's Tale* doesn't seem so far-fetched.

Consider a workforce stripped of its diversity, in which women's voices no longer make up half the conversation. As of 2019, women were on track to make up a majority of the college-educated labor force. Losing that level of talent not only wipes out thirty years of hard-won progress for women in the workforce and poses a human resources risk; it severely impacts workplace innovation, a crucial element for business survival. Instinctively we know that a collective of bright minds from varying perspectives makes better widgets, but research backs this up. A study released in 2019 by Accenture drew a direct line between equality and innovation, reporting that innovation is *six times higher* at organizations with more equal workplace cultures.

Lastly, and far from least important, we must imagine the long-term impact of the current state of affairs for working mothers on future generations. Research shows us clearly the effect of a mother's mental health on young children: preschool-aged children whose parents report stress during infancy are twice as prone to suffering from their own mental health issues by age three, and children of depressed parents who were tracked over a period of twenty years were found to be three times more at risk for mental health and substance abuse disorders.

We need to act fast to create better working conditions for moms, whether they work from home, in an office or institution, or a factory, to reverse the stunning trend of women exiting the workforce by the millions. We started the conversation, now it's time for women, families, employers, and policymakers to come together to demand and create a massive realignment and a new definition of working motherhood in America.

PART TWO

—

How Did We Get Here?

3

From Rosie the Riveter to #Girlboss

I've spent years fighting for gender parity in the workplace, yet I'm embarrassed to admit that it wasn't until researching this book that I got the full, clear picture of how women's role in the workforce took shape through the twentieth and twenty-first centuries. Understanding this is the key to seeing how the identities of "empowered woman in the workforce" and "the perfect mom" collided in a perfect storm. It's a story that's all at once fascinating, sobering, and—like most tales—obvious only in hindsight. I'm going to do a time-lapse version of this retelling so we can have the benefit of that hindsight as we exit the "where we've been" territory and move forward to the far more promising "where we're going."

RIGHT TO VOTE ≠ RIGHT TO WORK

The twentieth century saw women get off to a slow start in the workforce. In 1920, as the fight begun by first-wave feminists claimed victory in securing women the right to vote, only 8.3 million women over the age of fifteen worked outside the home. To put this in perspective, this was less than one-quarter of the labor force at that time. Most worked in domestic service; the few who did land factory jobs were paid 25 cents compared to 40 cents for men in the same jobs. The first generation of college-educated women entering the workforce found gainful employment only in "women's professions" like teaching and nursing.

From its inception, the modern workplace was antagonistic to mothers, because it simply was not available to them. In the prewar period, the women who worked were almost exclusively unmarried. There were laws in place which forbade married women from working (yes, really), and the expectation was that marriage—and, of course, motherhood—necessitated the woman's place in the house, taking care of domestic duties, and, eventually, caring for the children.

When the Great Depression hit in 1929, married women were officially blocked from finding work thanks to several restrictive public policies. For instance, the Economy Act of 1932 stipulated that only one family member could work for the government, keeping married women out of the only jobs available to them, such as teachers or librarians. The Franklin

Delano Roosevelt (FDR) administration launched the Works Progress Administration in 1935 to create much-needed relief jobs—but no relief was forthcoming for married women. Because recipients had to prove they were the "economic head of the household," any woman who had a physically able husband—whether he was employed or not—was automatically disqualified.

"WE CAN DO IT"

The landscape changed dramatically during World War II (1939–1945), as women stepped up to fill the millions of vacancies in the workforce left by men sent off to fight. Between 1940 and 1945, the number of women in the civilian workforce increased by fifty percent, rising to 18.6 million. Suddenly, these second-class Americans became celebrated wartime heroes, saving our economy from total collapse. One of the most iconic images of that era is that of Rosie the Riveter, an attractive fictional character in a bandana and rolled-up sleeves with a look of fierce determination on her face, featured on governmental propaganda posters affirming, "We Can Do It." Rosie boosted not just morale; women's wages saw healthy increases thanks to the wartime economy. It bears noting that women of color did not fare as well on the home front, as many of these "can do" white women workers said "won't do" when asked to work next to minority women on factory lines.

Women were so vital to the survival of the American economy that in 1942, first lady Eleanor Roosevelt convinced her husband, FDR, to create the first governmentally funded childcare facilities to help women manage their competing roles as workers and mothers. Seven centers were built, servicing 105,000 children, which of course did not come close to meeting the pressing needs of working mothers. But still, it was a start.

For all the beloved admiration showered on Rosie and the millions of women who filled crucial jobs to support the war effort, however, men's return at the end of the war also signaled the end of the boon for women in the workforce. If anything, we saw a rebound effect as traditional gender assumptions all but forced women back into the home. They were urged to return to their "rightful place" and laid off in large numbers from factory and office jobs to make way for men to reestablish their position as the family breadwinner.

To sweeten the transition—or, more accurately, to capitalize on the booming housing market in postwar America and tap into the consumer power of housewives—manufacturers in the 1950s invented scores of home products, appliances, and gadgets to enable women to be "empowered" in their rightful role as homemakers. This was the decade of automated washing machines (and ads showing cheerful housewives chirping, "My washdays are holidays now!") and Tupperware parties (a clever way for entrepreneurial women to maintain financial independence without having to leave the home). The message to women was broadcast loud and clear: Stay home and find fulfillment where you belong.

THE REAWAKENING OF THE FEMINIST MOVEMENT

By the sixties, however, millions of women yearned to return to the workforce, realizing that they were not, in fact, fulfilled in the domestic sphere. Betty Friedan's 1963 opus, *The Feminine Mystique*, gave those women a voice, criticizing the sentiment that a woman's place was in the home and that she should be fully satisfied by housework, marriage, and child-rearing. Friedan's book is credited with reinvigorating the stalled feminist movement, and second-wave feminism was born. Central to the fight for equality was achieving equality in the workplace through equal opportunity and equal pay. This was the frontier we needed to charge, with bravery and determination. And with second-wave feminists at the helm, charge it we did.

It's important to note that the goal of equal wages did not just pop up in the mid- to late-twentieth century. From the very beginning of the women's rights movement in this country, the demand for "equal pay for equal work" has been a feature, side by side with suffrage and the reform of divorce laws. The front page of the very first issue of Elizabeth Cady Stanton and Susan B. Anthony's newspaper, *Revolution*, published in 1868, stated that "We shall show that the ballot will secure for women equal place and equal wages in the world of work; that it will open to her the schools, colleges, professions, and all the opportunities and advantages of life . . ."

The National Organization for Women (NOW) launched in 1966 as the self-described grassroots arm of the women's

movement. Among their aims, outlined in their original statement of purpose, was to bring awareness to the declining status of women in the United States at that time, during which
almost half of all American women between ages eighteen
and sixty-five worked outside the home but the overwhelming
majority of them worked in low-paying jobs in administration,
sales, factories, or in domestic service roles. They sought to
close the wage gap which, at the time, earned women only
sixty percent of what men earned. Most notably, they fought
for ten years to get the Equal Rights Amendment (ERA) ratified. Though they got Congress to pass the bill in 1972, it was
never ratified by enough states to make it into law.

In 1971, Gloria Steinem, Patricia Carbine, and Elizabeth
Forsling Harris launched *Ms.* magazine, becoming the leading
voice of second-wave feminism. This, along with many other
advocacy efforts of these feminist leaders, burst open opportunities for women in the workplace. As a result, the percentage
of women working outside the home grew from twenty-seven
percent in 1960 to fifty-four percent in 1980. Second-wave feminism had become such a powerful force that in 1975, *Time*
magazine named "American Women" as their Man of the Year.

And since immersing myself in this work, I've become
fascinated by an alternate movement happening at the same
time as second-wave feminism came to the fore: the Wages for
Housework Campaign. In the early 1970s, the intersectional
feminists behind this movement argued that second-wave
feminists were narrowly focused on workplace equality and ig-

nored that women's work in the home, their domestic labor, had value. Housework, from child-rearing to tending to the family, was essential to a thriving economy and should be valued as such. The demands were simple and revolutionary: Acknowledge and value this labor through wages. Wages would not only recognize the unpaid work done at home, they would give women the economic and political value in the capitalist system to organize.

The movement lives on in various incarnations and they continue to advocate for valuing unpaid labor. It's fascinating to consider what would have happened today if the policies this movement was calling for had been instituted in light of research released by Oxfam showing that if American women made minimum wage for the work they did around the house and caring for relatives they would have earned $1.5 trillion in 2019. Globally, the value of that unpaid labor would have been close to $10.9 trillion.

In the years and decades since the rise of second-wave feminism, we saw impressive breakthroughs for women shattering the glass ceiling in a wide range of industries and sectors. In 1972, Katharine Graham became the first female CEO of a Fortune 500 company (*The Washington Post*); Geisha Williams put another crack in that ceiling in 2017 when she was named CEO of PG&E, making her the first female Latina CEO of a Fortune 500 company. In 1976, Barbara Walters broke the reliable mold of white men as news anchors, becoming the first female nightly news anchor in America. In 1981, we saw Sandra

Day O'Connor take her seat as the first female Supreme Court justice, and, of course, Kamala Harris became the first female vice president of the United States in 2021.

Four Public Policies That Advanced Women in the Workforce

- **The Equal Pay Act of 1963** prohibits gender-based wage discrimination in the United States. Signed by President John F. Kennedy as an amendment to the Fair Labor Standards Act, the bill was among the first laws in American history aimed at reducing gender discrimination in the workplace.

- **Title VII of the Civil Rights Act of 1964** is the gold standard for anti-discrimination, as it made it illegal for any workplace with fifteen or more employees to discriminate against anyone on the basis of race, sex, religion, or nationality. Additionally, the law prohibits employers from discriminating based on gender stereotyping. For instance, a newly married woman in her late twenties cannot be passed over for a promotion on the basis that she might one day soon become pregnant and need to take time off.

- **The Pregnancy Discrimination Act of 1978** forbade by law discrimination based on pregnancy with regard to any aspect of employment, from hiring to job assignments to promotions. The PDA helped to smooth the way for women to increasingly think of their jobs as careers that might extend through and past whatever interruption might be associated with pregnancy. In practice, of course, women were still routinely held back by the realities of pregnancy and childbirth for all the reasons you already well know.

- **The Family and Medical Leave Act (FMLA)** was signed into law by President Bill Clinton in 1993, giving parents the right to take time off to care for a new baby or adopted child without having to worry they will lose their job. While this is a step in the right direction, it's important to note that the FMLA does not guarantee *paid leave*—just the fact that you can take unpaid leave up to twelve weeks without fear of repercussions. As of the writing of this book, Congress is debating President Biden's Build Back Better Plan, which initially proposed twelve weeks paid leave for all new parents. At the time of writing, a bill providing four weeks of paid leave was passed in the House but had not yet been voted on by the Senate.

THE "MODERN" WOMAN

Policy changes and employment statistics are one way to track women's advancement in the labor force. Another way to track the perception of what makes a woman "empowered" through the decades is by examining the workplace personas and values we hold up as ideal.

To my mind, there is no better place to start the story of how the Big Lie took shape than with the publication of Helen Gurley Brown's 1982 book, *Having It All*. As the author of *Sex and the Single Girl* and editor of *Cosmopolitan* magazine for thirty-two years, Brown was a major voice in championing the sexual revolution of the sixties and seventies. In *Having It All*, she took the "go for it" manifesto a step further into the workplace, urging women to go for more money, more love, more sex, more power. While terribly dated now (including advice on sleeping with your boss and cultivating "a touch of anorexia nervosa to maintain your ideal weight"), at the time, it spoke to a generation filled with women who were eager to "have it all," whatever that took.

It's probably no coincidence that Brown's book was published when the shudder-inducing commercial for Enjoli perfume was all the rage. In case you don't know of it, the commercial I'm referring to was for a perfume made by Charles of the Ritz that featured a hot blond Supermom who we see transitioning from a business suit into "home-cooking clothes" and then a slinky evening gown (or nightgown, hard to say), singing: "*I can bring home the bacon, fry it up in a pan. And never ever let you forget you're a man . . . I can work 'til five o'clock, come home and read you* Tickety-Tock *. . . 'cause I'm a woman . . .*" The tagline: "Enjoli. The 8-hour perfume for the 24-hour woman."

I'll just leave that right there.

The eighties saw the rise of women-acting-like-men in order to get ahead in the workplace. Think Sigourney Weaver in *Working Girl*, a tough-as-nails businesswoman with a taste for power suits; or Candice Bergen's character on the eponymous hit series *Murphy Brown*, an unmarried, sharp-witted investigative journalist who made no bones about being hyper-ambitious. Diane Keaton's character J. C. Wiatt in 1987's *Baby Boom* encapsulated in no uncertain terms the "this or that" choice between big-time career and family. A power-driven management consultant known as "The Tiger Lady," Wiatt is unwittingly bequeathed a baby girl upon a distant relative's death. As the movie progresses, we watch her ping-ponging from awkward to frantic trying to make peace between her power-hungry persona at work and her newfound responsibilities as a mother. In the end, she realizes she can't have both, so she leaves corporate America and the big city for a sweeter, quieter life with her daughter in Vermont, where she sets up an at-home baby food business. No need for interpretation.

By 1985, the percentage of women between the ages of twenty-five and forty-four in the labor force had rocketed to an impressive seventy-one percent. The census that year showed that more than half of young mothers with preschoolers were participating in the workforce. Images of working mothers were everywhere in popular media, most notably the full-time attorney, wife, and mother of five, Claire Huxtable, on *The Cosby Show*—a shining beacon of having it all. While her obstetrician husband cheerfully shared in the domestic responsibilities, in hindsight, one has to wonder: Who was really doing the laundry, figuring out what to make for dinner, and taking the kids to their various appointments if both parents worked in such big jobs? That element was conveniently obscured.

Of all the television moms in the '90s, it was Jennifer Aniston's character Rachel Green on *Friends* that struck me the most. I mean, here was this single, working mom with a baby . . . who we almost never saw on-screen other than for moments of "aww isn't she cute" or brief hilarity. Who was taking care of the kid? How in the world did Rachel manage to work full-time (with travel!), work out (wtf with that body?), take care of a baby, and still have picture-perfect hair? At least on *Sex and the City* we saw a decent amount of spit-up on Miranda's power suit.

Rounding the corner into the twenty-first century, the ethos of women navigating a male-dominated workforce still holds. The best-selling career strategy *Nice Girls Don't Get the Corner Office*, written by Lois Frankel in 2004, urged women to "quit being a girl" and get ahead by figuring out the "unspoken rules." And then, of course, there is Sheryl Sandberg's 2013 women's self-empowerment tome, *Lean In: Women, Work, and the Will to Lead*, which defined for women what it means to get ahead at work by taking risks and rooting out the internal impediments that hold them back. While "Lean In" has become a ubiquitous term, Sandberg did come under fire for what many felt was elitist and out of touch with the actual realities of working motherhood. But it's undeniable that the book was essential to sparking conversations and moving the ball down the field.

On the heels of *Lean In* came the #Girlboss brand of feminism dictating how women should kick ass in the workplace. Originally coined by CEO of Nasty Gal Sophia Amoruso in her memoir by the same name, a "girlboss" is a young woman leader who does not *ask* to be in charge; she takes the reins—without apology and with a winning smile—from the patriarchy that lorded it over her on her way up. She is an apex predator yet, as the infantilizing moniker suggests, relatable and unintimidating. Fueled by YouTube, Twitter, and TikTok feeds, the girlboss consumes and spits back out the bits and pieces of feminism that best serve her capitalist agenda, all in the name of striking a blow for equality in the workplace.

Like me, I bet a lot of women at one time wore (or aspired to wear) "girlboss" as a badge of honor. As misguided as the whole culture was, I know there are a lot of women looking back on that hustle today with a little nostalgia. The problem (okay, a few of the problems) with the girlboss model is that it was ruthless, it was unattainable, it was hypocritical. It made it every woman's job to be exceptional instead of collectively fighting the racism and sexism we all need to be facing together. Frankly, it's part of why we are here. But the biggest problem with the girlboss mythology is that it is exactly that: a myth. If we could just waltz into the workforce and take the equality we've spent the better part of a century fighting for, I kind of think we would have by now.

Despite all their empowerment and advancement, what workforce powerhouses like Rosie the Riveter, shoulder pad—

clad Tiger Ladies, and leaned-in girlbosses overlooked was the counternarrative running in the background that was insidiously rising to the fore at the exact same time, putting them on a collision course that would eventually blow apart their ambition, dreams, and notion of equality.

4

The Counternarrative: Women at Home

If you look back over the last few pages chronicling the decades-long march toward equality undertaken by the feminist movement, popular business psychology, and public policy, you'll notice one word that is all but absent: mothers. In our fight for equality, the "mother" part of women's identities got left behind.

With the exception of Eleanor Roosevelt, and one chapter in *Lean In* that urges women to demand more help at home (as if we are all in heteronormative relationships and demanding your partner do more actually works . . .), no one in the mix of lobbyists and authors and lawmakers threw a yellow flag on the field signaling that equality for women in the workplace without equality in the domestic sphere was a recipe for disaster.

It's basic math: Take two people. Put both in demanding jobs with full-time hours. All things being equivalent in terms of education, skill, and ability, they are on equal footing. Now add an entire second job to one of their plates. Literally, an entire second job that that person is meant to do *on top of their existing job.* The game is lost before it's even begun, because there is no chance for equality in the workplace with the odds stacked against them like that. They are almost immediately sidelined by discrimination, burnout, financial constraints, and overwhelm caused by an extreme output of cognitive labor.

We are operating in a system that has set us up to fail.

While the feminist march for equality in the workplace drove on, two other forces gained momentum as the twentieth century progressed: the rise of intensive parenting and the mythology of the "ideal mother."

THE PRESSURE COOKER OF PERFECT PARENTING

I was walking home from work when I got a call from my sister, Keshma, a busy ob-gyn in Georgia and mother of three kids, whom I don't get to catch up with very often. I picked it up, excited for a quick catch-up with one of my favorite people during the rest of my walk, and all I heard on the other end was "OH MY GOD, Resh . . . ARGGHHH!!!" (Did I mention she's a character? She's endlessly entertaining.)

Settling in for what I was sure was going to be a funny story, I laughed and said, "Haha, okay . . . I'm listening."

But no funny story was forthcoming. Instead, to my surprise, my sister was actually in tears. I stopped in my tracks; my sister delivers eighty babies a week, she never melts down.

"What's wrong?" I asked, getting scared. "Who's sick?"

"No, no," she assured me. "Kaiden just called me to say he got accepted onto the travel soccer team at school. The TRAVEL SOCCER team. That means two days a week now I have to drive him to god knows where and wait there and . . . honestly, I'm just going to lose it. I know he really wants this and I should be happy and grateful that my kid is thriving, but how many activities is enough? Jesus, these kids are eight years old!"

I get it. Oh, man, do I get it.

Here I am, the author of a book about eradicating perfectionism, and just like my sister, I still fall prey to the pressure to optimize every opportunity for my kids. I feel too guilty not to nurture every passing interest my kids have (*don't stifle their creativity . . . !*), or cultivate a potential gift (*he's got such good rhythm . . . maybe drum lessons?*). While I know it's a staple of privilege being a parent who can afford these fancy classes, I feel the pressure to get them into the "right" classes to set them up for life success (*Spanish at age five? Of course, it's the language of the future*) and show up for every moment (*Come be the parent reader for story time at school? Of course!*).

In this age of intensive parenting, I'm hard pressed to say whether the pressure comes more from the judgments I feel from outside sources—articles, glossy Instagram posts, the looks I interpret as judgment from other moms who are doing it better—or whether it's just my perfection drive whispering that if I miss one tiny opportunity to enhance my kids' creativity, intelligence, or social lives, I'll screw them up forever. I'm going to go out on a limb and say it's the latter, as women have the drive for perfection baked into them at an early age (more on this in chapter 6).

Parenting, as cultural critics like Robert Putnam and others have remarked, has become a competitive sport. Moms and dads, but particularly moms, jump onto the field to engage in what sociologist Annette Lareau described as "concerted cultivation" of children. Affluent and middle-class families spend thousands of dollars on enriching the cognitive and social functions of their children outside of school time, driving a deeper wedge between the classes as working-class families have steadily less time and resources to spend on their kids.

But it's not just extracurricular activities we're talking about here. The expectation is that we—or at the very least, capable and trustworthy caregivers—are with our children every minute of the day when they are not in school, cultivating their potential so they can have a "résumé" that gives them a leg up on other kids vying to get into the best colleges. Judith Treas, University of California, Irvine, professor of sociology and coauthor of a study that analyzed the caregiving hours of parents across eleven countries between 1965 and 2012, confirmed, "The time parents spend with children is regarded as critical for positive cognitive, behavioral and academic outcome." On a slightly lighter but no less pressurized note, economists

Garey Ramey and Valerie A. Ramey of the University of California, San Diego, call this new kind of intensive parenting "the rug rat race."

In response to these rising pressures, the number of hours that college-educated parents (read: moms) spend with their children has doubled since the early 1980s. Yes, that's right: *doubled*. They spend more of that time than their parents ever did talking things over, sharing activities, and teaching. But dads are mostly insulated from this development. Working mothers today spend as much time with their children as stay-at-home mothers did in the 1970s. This, on top of the American workforce expectation that the "ideal worker" put in world record–breaking hours without showing any signs of outside distractions.

Cue the life crisis waiting to happen . . .

MOTHERHOOD AND APPLE PIE

The vision of the "ideal mother" coalesced pretty much around the same time that women were pushed out of the postwar workforce and back into the domestic sphere. The happy homemakers of the 1950s raised the kids and tended the house while their husbands went off to work. In advertisement after advertisement, sitcom after sitcom, the ideal mom was brimming with love and the apple-pie promise of the American Dream.

All this was deeply enmeshed with the politics of the era. As the Cold War gripped the country in fear, the typical American home became a shining symbol of democracy. The G.I. Bill made it possible for more Americans than ever to own homes, promoting the picture-perfect nuclear family as the epitome of patriotism. As William Levitt, the developer behind Long Island's affordable, whites-only community Levittown famously said, "No man who owns his own house and lot can be a Communist. He has too much to do."

Here's when things really get cooking. At the same point that Gloria Steinem and other activists ushered in the second wave of feminism and women were empowered to make strides toward advancement in the workplace, the seeds of mom guilt were also being planted. In order to keep cracking through that glass ceiling, women had to take pains to hide their mothering so as to not jeopardize the feminist momentum. On the surface, we were liberated and empowered . . . the veritable embodiment of bringing home the bacon and frying it up in a pan! Behind the scenes, however, small tears were starting to appear in the enticing manifesto of "having it all." By the time sociologist Arlie Hochschild published her seminal book, *The Second Shift: Working Parents and the Revolution at Home,* in 1989, detailing the domestic work shouldered mainly by mothers at the end of a full workday, those small tears had already grown into gaping holes.

The tapestry really started to unravel in the nineties, as the threads of mom judgment began to pull at the seams. We saw the emergence of the power struggle known as the "Mommy Wars," pitting working mothers against stay-at-home mothers.

The divide between the haves and have nots, in this case, came down to who still believed "having it all" was possible and who chose one in favor of the other. A 1990 article in *Newsweek* titled "Mommy vs. Mommy" underscored the divergence and divide playing out between women and, for many, within themselves. "This conflict is played out against a backdrop of frustration, insecurity, jealousy and guilt," the writer observed. "And because the enemies should be allies, the clash is poignant."

WHEN WORLDS COLLIDE

As we rounded the corner into the twenty-first century, the age of intensive parenting dawned, and we were officially done for. Now, not only did we have to present ourselves at work as unencumbered, relentlessly committed workers, we also had to raise perfectly organic-fed, trilingual, karate-kicking, ballet-twirling, socially confident children—and smile happily for Instagram posts while doing it. As Elizabeth Weiss wrote in her article "Selling the Myth of the Ideal Mother" in the *New Yorker*, "Our current parenting culture of taxing schedules, organic snacks, and profound emotional involvement— motherhood as a contact sport—pressures women to perform to impossible standards."

In a paper published in the *Russell Sage Foundation Journal of the Social Sciences*, the authors noted how the demands of today's top earners—who, according to their research, work fifty hours or more per week—conflict so profoundly with the vision of the ideal mother. "The 'ideal worker' is someone who is available to clients and supervisors at all hours of the day or night, is able to travel or relocate for work, and prioritizes career success over family or leisure," they wrote. "This is hard to reconcile with the stereotype of the ideal mother, a mother who is available to her family at all hours of the day or night, is able to travel or relocate to support her children's enrichment activities and prioritizes family over career success."

But women don't need experts to tell us what we already know about our reality.

REBELS WITHOUT A FRYING PAN

This takes us all the way up to today, when a 2016 comedy called *Bad Moms* resonated with millions of mothers who were cracking mightily under the strain. Reviews from the critics on the film were mixed, but women didn't care. They flocked to the theaters and turned the movie into a cultural anthem for perfectly imperfect mothers everywhere.

At the heart of the story are three moms who had just had *enough*. Enough of the sugar police. Enough of the mom-shaming of bringing store-bought doughnuts to a school bake sale or hitting the drive-thru at Arby's. Enough of the expectations that their kids should be perfectly molded athletes, scholars, and citizens—not to mention social superstars. Enough of the PTA politics dominated by hyper-competitive, perfection-driven women who are supposed to be their sisters-in-arms but instead are the punitive force of judgment. Like moms all across America, I cheered out loud when one of the lead characters gave a rousing speech at the PTA election encouraging the rest of the moms to abandon the lunacy of perfect parenting, once and for all.

Of course, we don't live on a Hollywood stage set, and we can't wrap up the overwhelming story of how working women found themselves where they are in a neat run time of 101 minutes, not including credits. So, what can we do?

The pandemic, as we well know by now, blew out of hiding the impossible conflation of intensive parenting, cultural expectations of moms, and the demands that came along with women's advancement in the workplace. It's a trifecta that has set us up to fail, but COVID-19 has given us a once-in-a-generation opportunity to reconfigure the equation.

PART THREE

—

Paid in Full:
How We Get There

5

The Four Forces of Change

It's time that leaders admit once and for all that the workplace does not work for women with children. And that this silent marginalization is treacherous for the mental health of their women workers, for their companies' bottom lines, their ability to survive in the post-pandemic reality, and the viability of the American economy.

It's time we as women stop having to hide our motherhood or choose between motherhood and ambition because our culture praises us for each separately but punishes us for it when combined. It's time for us to move from rage to power, to stop trying to figure out how to adapt in a workplace that is built for men and to get loud and tactical about how the workplace can adapt to us. It's time for lawmakers in our country to step up and for cultural influencers to change the grossly outdated narrative around women, work, and motherhood. It's time for the institutions that have sidelined working mothers in ways both obvious and hidden to Pay Up!

These changes are no longer wishes or nice ideas. They are critical. As we look ahead to how we repair and reassemble the scorched earth exposed by the pandemic, we find ourselves at a historic inflection point. The actions every single one of us as workers, employers, policymakers, and family members take—or don't take—will determine the future of the labor force, the economy, and the social fabric of our country as we know it.

The plan laid out in the coming chapters calls on the four powerful forces that need to work in tandem to generate the seismic shifts women in the workforce need: employers and business leaders, policymakers, cultural perceptions, and women themselves. Yes, we need a wholesale revision of our public policies as they relate to mothers in the labor force, and women and our allies are fighting mightily for those as I write this. But we in the private sector need to step up just as powerfully. We need to reimagine how our workplaces are constructed and give women more support, choices, and control over their lives. We need to root out the embedded cultural perception of motherhood and caregiving and redefine it, so that the perceptions and expectations in the workplace and inside the home naturally recalibrate. We must reconsider the value (or lack thereof) we place on parenting and running a household and compensate women for the unpaid labor they do that fuels our economy and literally creates and sustains the next generation.

This is a call to arms that goes way beyond redistributing housework, getting women into the C-suites—even beyond "social safety net" legislation proposed by President Biden. This is an all-hands effort; we need everyone to do their part to generate the revolution that women in the workplace so urgently need and deserve.

THE PLAN: EMPOWER, EDUCATE, REVISE, ADVOCATE

At the center of this revolution is us—the working women who refuse to sit idly one moment more as the dueling demands of our identities collide and our ambitions, dreams, and mental health are laid to waste. This plan is both for and about us, emboldening us from the inside out to alter the landscape on which we work and live.

EMPOWER

When I wrote *Brave, Not Perfect*, I was still in the throes of promoting the feminist propaganda of having it all via leaning in. I still wholeheartedly believe that empowering and taking personal responsibility for advancing ourselves matters. But where I got it wrong is that it is not the *only* thing that matters. Without also changing the system in which we operate, we'll keep landing in the same pressure cooker of responsibilities, expectations, and impossible ideals that we've been frying ourselves to a crisp trying to meet.

This isn't all on us. Will giving up the "nice girl" behaviors, taking risks (that one is on me), and learning to decode the unwritten rules so we can work them to our advantage get us ahead in the workplace?

Yes, probably.

Will that myopic approach get us ahead in life? Absolutely not.

We've made the mistake for far too long of leaning into our work while hiding the fact that we were also leaning into the double shift of running our families, home, and personal lives. Career success is absolutely worthy and admirable; but redistributing the lean so we can sanely hold up in both arenas *with the full support and respect of our employers, families, and government* is the actual prize.

What you'll find in chapter 6 are not more blithe suggestions for self-care. I think we've had enough of those! Instead, these are baseline, scientifically proven strategies to empower the initial force—you—so that you can take steps to change both your reality *and* the reality in which you work and live.

EDUCATE

It's one thing to say we need to make global, systemic changes in our workplaces. Yes, we do. But what does that mean, really? What kind of changes? What do they look like, specifically, and how exactly do we make them?

Here's where the "educate" part comes in. Based on studies and emerging best practices, chapter 7 offers an in-depth reimagining of the workplace. It is a call out to employers, but it is also for us, as women in the workforce, to become knowledgeable advocates for new workplace practices and give us tools to illuminate for our individual employers how (and more importantly, why) they can and should implement these changes.

REVISE

The third force of change that needs to be mobilized is amorphous, yet pervasive: the ridiculously outdated cultural perceptions around women, work, and motherhood, which we'll tackle head-on in chapter 8.

In their 2019 bestseller *Burnout*, authors Emily and Amelia Nagoski popularized philosopher Kate Manne's "Human Giver Syndrome," the societal convention that women are expected to be infinitely selfless, sacrificing their time, bodies, and affection in service to others at every moment. The archetypal image of the "perfect mother" as one who gives and sacrifices all that she is for her children cannot possibly fit into the same human form as the "ideal worker" who dedicates herself to her full-time job fully and without distraction.

Why focus on mothers, specifically?

In order to generate the seismic shifts needed to reshape the future of work for all women, we must start by reshaping the landscape for working mothers. Why are we any more important than women in the workforce who don't have children? To be crystal clear: We aren't more important—but we are far, *far* less valued in the workplace, and that is the weak spot for the future of gender equality, the future of our economy, and the future of all women who are told, directly or indirectly, that they must be unencumbered by home life responsibilities in order to succeed. It's not a coincidence that eighty percent of CEOs have wives who are not employed and work full-time raising their children, managing the household, and running the family enterprise.

We must support and invest in the women who do double duty flying the flag of gender equality in the workplace and then go home to do the invisible work that keeps our social fabric and economic ecosystem intact. Whether we are one of them now, perhaps one day want to be, or have no intention of ever being, we need to fight for the rights of working mothers because we are, in essence, fighting for *every* woman's right to have control over their choices about work and motherhood (as opposed to either/or), their schedules, and their lives.

But first, we all—yes, working mothers included—need to root out the implicit biases that we don't even know we harbor and that perpetuate outdated gender roles, assumptions, and stereotypes and revise our beliefs about "the perfect mother" and "ideal worker."

ADVOCATE

As political activist Emma Goldman said in the early twentieth century, "Women need not always keep their mouths shut and their wombs open. No real social change has ever been brought about without a revolution . . . revolution is but thought carried into action."

This truth still holds. As I write this, my newsfeed is inundated daily with analyses and arguments for and against paid leave and other public policies that are crucial for working women. The government is the final force of change that we need to step up. Yet with all the whiplash reversals of proposed bills and confusing commentary, many of us don't even know what we are fighting for. My friend Mara went to a yoga class with the instructor she'd been going to for years when the instructor suddenly announced that she would be canceling the class going forward because, "I can't afford my babysitter anymore and my husband is a jerk. I'm sorry I'm letting you all down." Mara pulled her aside after class to ask whether she knew about President Biden's bill to make childcare more affordable. She looked at Mara very confused. "I thought all of those bills were just about building roads and bridges," she said. "I didn't even know that the government could help me."

Yes, it can. And it must. Chapter 9 will give us all a bottom-line primer on what's needed, why, and what you can do to generate and contribute to the revolution that our sisters-in-arms began a full century ago.

6

EMPOWER: Changing Our Reality from Within

To be truly visionary we have to root our imagination in our concrete reality while simultaneously imagining possibilities beyond that reality.

—bell hooks

Let me be crystal clear right up front: This is *not* all on you. Feminist activists have long been beating the drum that women are NOT the ones to blame for being unable to scale the heights of success with the same nimble speed as men while managing a full home life—while also, of course, staying sane and in fabulous shape.

I won't insult you by suggesting that if you just take a mental health day once in a while, amp yourself up with Instagram motivational quotes, and "learn how to say no" you'll ace the battle of achieving equality (and sanity) in your workplace and your home life.

What I am suggesting, though—based on many years of research and work as a women's empowerment leader and experience working right alongside hundreds of women business leaders—is that there are some baseline strategies that can and do shore up our well-being. Empowering ourselves on mental, physical, and emotional levels gives us the grit we need to carve new inroads for ourselves in our workplace, culture, and policies.

I promise, this isn't another exhaustive list of things you need to do—we're all already overloaded, and none of us need to add one more thing to our agendas. This is far more fundamental than that. What you'll find here are three primary facets of empowerment with practical, manageable steps:

1. Establish Baseline Non-Negotiables
2. Set Tangible Boundaries
3. Put the Perfection Thing to Rest Already

These three, set in motion in tandem, will enable you to reclaim your power, bit by bit.

ESTABLISH BASELINE NON-NEGOTIABLES

A quick browse through any women's magazine will reveal dozens of strategies to improve your well-being. The majority of them are wonderful—believe me, I, too, would love to exercise for thirty minutes four to five times a week, do a cleanse, spend quality time with my family and friends, enjoy a rejuvenating hike outdoors to increase my vitamin D levels, grind flaxseeds to make homemade smoothies chock-full of greens and fiber, and meditate for twenty minutes twice daily.

The problem with that list isn't any of those suggestions. It's the word "AND" that connects them. If our insanely packed lives juggling work and home responsibilities actually allowed us to do all these things, we wouldn't be where we are.

That's why I've whittled this down to the three that science (and common sense) tells us are the most crucial for filling our tank.

GET ENOUGH SLEEP

The work of turning the ship to go against a strong tide—whether we are talking about speaking up for what you need at work or setting new boundaries at home—takes stamina, bravery, patience, and full-on grit. Before we can even imagine conjuring up those forces within ourselves, we have to fill our tank. As Arianna Huffington, the global media leader who wrote a best-selling book about the importance of sleep, once told me, *we cannot swim against the tide if we are exhausted.*

That's why the straight-up strategy of getting enough sleep comes first. It's the foundation that needs to be put in place to enable all the others. The Mayo Clinic is clear on the repercussions of sleep deprivation, ranging from depression to inability to focus and think clearly. A 2007 study out of Duke University shows that consistent lack of sleep causes us to underestimate possible negative outcomes of our decisions. In other words, no sleep means impaired judgment. I don't know about you, but I've never made a single good decision when I'm tired.

Sleep deprivation is directly linked to increased risk of depression and anxiety. The Cleveland Clinic reports that lack of sleep can lead to long-term and serious conditions and illnesses such as diabetes, heart disease, stroke, and impaired immunity. If you think you don't have time or bandwidth now, just add in one of those ailments and you'll have a whole new appreciation for why getting enough sleep matters.

Study after study tells us that seven to nine hours a night is what we need to function optimally. If you make one change and one change only, let it be establishing hard-core boundaries around your bedtime and wake time. Seriously. The best thing I did this year was get myself a WHOOP, which is a wearable device that measures my sleep and recovery. It has ruined my social life because red wine is horrible for good sleep and put an end to my Netflix and ice cream date night with myself, but I am vigilant about my sleep now.

Will some things not get done? Probably. Will the entire family enterprise collapse if you don't get that online order in for new sheets for your son before the sale ends at midnight? I'm guessing no.

The rest of your household will adjust to your fixed schedule faster than you think. The key is to make it non-negotiable and—equally important—for you to not apologize for fulfilling an essential human need. If you're not quite ready to claim seven to nine hours of sleep for your own sake, remind your family that a sleep-deprived woman is 100 percent guaranteed to be a less present, less capable, less pleasant mother and partner to be around.

They'll get the picture, fast.

HEALTH FIRST. PERIOD.

A 2015 survey conducted by HealthyWoman and *Working Mother* magazine revealed that women prioritize the management of healthcare in the following order:

1. Children
2. Pets
3. Elder relatives
4. Significant other or spouse
5. Themselves

You see the problem here.

I'm not here to give you the standard "put your own oxygen mask on first so you can help others" speech. Yes, your well-being is crucial for the sustenance of your family. But in that argument, we are once again focusing on items 1–4 in the list above. It's #5 we need to take a beat to work on here.

According to Ovarian Cancer Action, more than a quarter of women said they prioritize work over making necessary doctor appointments. A third said that looking after their family came before anything else. We don't think twice about scheduling doctor appointments for our children or ailing parents, but when it comes to our own, we're either too busy or we feel too guilty. Not to put too fine a point on it, but prioritizing everyone above ourselves can be deadly. A study of more than half a million women funded by the American Cancer Society stated that skipping even one scheduled mammogram before a breast cancer diagnosis increases a woman's chance of dying. Senator Amy Klobuchar, who herself skipped a mammogram in 2020 and then discovered she had (thankfully treatable) breast cancer, observed that since the pandemic hit, so many adults are still juggling childcare, remote work, and aging parents that self-care gets put on the back burner.

But first, we need to put prioritizing our health back on the front burner—STAT. How can you possibly feel empowered if you're in pain, rundown, insufficiently nourished, or sick? Moving yourself to the top of that list starts with reinstituting some baseline healthy habits like eating decently well and getting some exercise. You don't need to go full-on organic gourmet or sign up for CrossFit six days a week to fulfill those vital requirements. Just educate yourself on the absolute basics and do what you can do—but do *something*.

Second, take your medical maintenance seriously. You wouldn't dare skip your kids' yearly checkups or tell your elderly parent that the nagging pain in their lower belly is nothing to worry about. Their health is non-negotiable, and yours needs to be, too.

Why put your own oxygen mask on first? So you can *breathe*. It's really that simple.

LEAN OUT OF WORK AND INTO YOURSELF ONCE IN A WHILE

There is a woman who is the parent of one of my son's friends—let's call her Tanika and her son Jared—whom I have never, not once, gotten to talk about anything other than her kids. Tanika and I live in the same neighborhood and have mutual friends, and each and every time I see her, she steers the conversation straight to what the boys' teacher assigned that day, what my kids were dressing up as for Halloween, or another parenting detail. During the most intense part of the lockdown, I ran into her in line at the supermarket and I asked her how she was holding up. Her immediate answer, "It's hard for Jared not to see his friends, but he's getting by."

I have a suspicion this is not because Tanika has nothing else to talk about, but because she's fallen into the trap of seeing herself *only* as a parent. Her identity as a person is so intertwined with her role as a caregiver that she's obscured her value as an individual. Or, to put it another way, she's so immersed in parenting that she's lost sight of herself.

> *"I think my mother taught me what not to do. She put us first, always, sometimes to the detriment of herself. She encouraged me not to do that. She'd say being a good mother isn't all about sacrificing; it's really investing and putting yourself higher on your priority list."*
>
> MICHELLE OBAMA

There's a reason why the global wellness industry is valued at $4.2 trillion and the number of searches on Google for "self-care" has doubled since 2015. Leaning out of work and into self-care—in whatever form feeds you, even in small doses—has been shown again and again in studies to keep us physically, mentally, and emotionally healthy. It has been clinically proven to reduce anxiety and stress, improve concentration and sharpen cognition, mitigate frustration, boost energy, and more. It's the ticket to everything from resilience to weight loss, increased productivity to better sex.

When it comes to mental health, self-care is not a luxury. If we are seeking to mitigate the burnout that has been consuming women for so long, we need to start by claiming even the smallest amounts of time to do our part from within. Every. Bit. Counts.

So lean out of being a caregiver once in a while and into being a caretaker of yourself. I'm not proposing neglect of your family here. Just a slight recalculation of who gets your attention, support, and nurturing 100 percent of the time.

SET TANGIBLE BOUNDARIES

There's nothing worse than feeling like you have no control over your time or sense of personal boundaries. Research proves this loss of autonomy and sense of control over our own choices is directly linked to higher levels of stress that can have destructive effects.

As with any change, we are more likely to succeed when we start with smaller, less intimidating actions. It's like a muscle we build. That's why the first place to start in setting boundaries is at home—where the stakes are not as high and where, unfortunately, the dynamic can often feel personally stacked against us. Most specifically in the dreaded division of chores.

In the 2006 movie *The Break-Up*, starring Jennifer Aniston and Vince Vaughn, there's a scene in which the lead characters—whose relationship, as the title suggests, is falling apart—are having what feels like their millionth fight about imbalances in household chores. Or, more accurately, how Vaughn's character, Gary, refuses to do pretty much anything other than open a beer when he gets home so he can "relax" after work. Despite her own full workdays, Aniston's character, Brooke, plans and executes every detail of a dinner party without any help from Gary, who was unwilling to do even the bare minimum of setting the table. After everyone leaves and they face a mountain of dirty dishes that Gary has no interest in helping clean up, an exasperated Brooke screams (to the silent cheers of enraged women everywhere), "I want you to *want* to do the dishes!"

Gary yells back, "No one *wants* to do the dishes."

A Media Callout

An overwhelming body of research confirms that children's perceptions of gender are influenced by movies and television they are exposed to. All of us—media executives and consumers alike—have an obligation to help shape better beliefs about women and division of responsibilities at home for the next generation. What kind of content are we creating and consuming, and what messages is it sending our kids about what roles they should play and how parenting responsibilities should be divided at home? How can we as parents help our kids interpret and analyze what they see?

The reality is that they're both right. As Gary said, no one *wants* to dive into a mess of sticky, dirty dishes after a long day. But to Brooke's point, *someone* has to wash the dishes, and make the food, and do the laundry—why does it always have to be her? Why doesn't Gary want to be an equal partner in the work it takes to run a household?

I'm not here to theorize about how we can "fix" our partners or suggest ways to get them to do more at home. Would it be great if every partner stepped right up to do a fully equal share of the invisible and emotional work of running a home and family life? Of course. Believe me, I'd love to stop fighting with my husband about who tracks when we're out of Cheerios or pauses their remote workday when our toddler yells from the bathroom that someone needs to come wipe his butt. But these are deeply ingrained norms we're talking about, and we all need to do our part to change our entire culture so that yes, everyone wants to *want* to do their part.

Having said all that, one simple way we can begin to change how the systemic inequities and expectations play out in our own homes and reclaim our power is by not only setting boundaries of who does what at home, but also *sticking to them*.

I'll show you what I mean.

Nihal and I came to an agreement that I would take the morning shift with the kids and he would do the early evening shift. At 6 p.m., when it was his shift, I'd go into our bedroom either to work or take a little time for myself to regroup before the evening bedtime brigade began. Invariably, Nihal would call my name from the living room while he was juggling the two kids and ask me, "Could you just . . ." Could I just quickly change the baby's diaper while he helped Shaan with his homework. Could I just see who's at the door? Could I just heat up a fast bottle?

For a while I'd get pissed off. So now I was not only doing the morning, but part of his night responsibilities, too? I got tired of yelling about it (and I'm sure he did, too), so now, when the nighttime routine begins, I just leave. I walk around the block. I go to the gym. I make a dinner date with friends. Sometimes I go to a bar and sit by myself with a drink and a book.

"Can you just . . . ?" Nope. I can't, because I'm not there. So now Nihal has no choice but to somehow make his evening shift work. And you know what? *He did.* Did he do it exactly as I would have done? No. Fairly often Shaan post-bath is wearing the bottoms of one set of pajamas and the top of another. But this comes right back to the strategy of letting good enough be good enough and hanging up my Supermom martyr cape.

Coming up with who does what on the "chore wheel" is the easy part. Not swooping in to take over whatever part of the wheel isn't in our domain—even if some things fall between the cracks—is the bigger challenge. So yes, divide the chores. Set the boundaries of what isn't yours to do. And then *don't do it.*

PUT THE PERFECTION THING TO REST ALREADY

Seriously. It's time.

Besides eating into our time, sense of life satisfaction, and overall happiness, and sapping any sense of empowerment (because, really, who achieves perfection, ever??), perfectionism has a crippling effect on our mental health. It is directly linked to depression, anxiety, and—in extreme cases—increased rates of suicide.

In my book *Brave, Not Perfect,* I outlined the underlying and insidious reason why women are so gripped by perfection. In a nutshell: Boys are raised to be and rewarded for being brave, while girls are raised to be and rewarded for being neat, clean, obedient, and pleasing—in other words, perfect. With the belief ingrained in us that doing everything "right" and pleasing others is the key to being worthy, we grow up to be women who are driven to do every last little thing to everyone's utmost satisfaction. Add in the societal expectation of women as the ultimate sacrificial caregivers and you see how we ended up in the crosshairs.

THE PERFECT GIVER

Take Michelle, for instance. Michelle, forty-eight, lives with her blended family that includes her husband, two stepsons ages fourteen and sixteen, and her two biological daughters ages nine and thirteen. "I kid you not," she told me. "I think I spend at least half my time thinking about how to keep everyone happy. Not just happy—it's like I need them to be happy *at all times*, otherwise I've failed."

For Michelle, keeping her family happy meant not just meeting their needs, but anticipating them. That encompassed everything from ordering a cake for her stepson's birthday that she remembered him mentioning six months earlier, making an appointment for her daughter to get her hair styled before her best friend's bat mitzvah the following week, taking her husband's shirts to the tailor to get the loose buttons secured so they don't fall off and finding his favorite pair of reading glasses he was upset that he'd lost somewhere in the house, downloading the forms for her other stepson that he needed to fill out by Friday in order to play football that season, and more. "I know I go overboard, but I get such a hit of satisfaction when I've nailed it," she explained.

I know exactly what she means. There is a distinct gratification I get from being the end-all-be-all detail coordinator in my house. When we are going on a road trip, I pack all my stuff as well as the kids'. Invariably, we will get in the car and Nihal will ask me, "Did you bring Shaan's Froggie?" And with a twisted pleasure and smug disdain, I look at him and say yes. *Yes, of course I remembered Froggie.*

I read a story not long ago about a mom who was taking care of her sick child. The baby had just fallen asleep on her, and of course, that was the moment the mom desperately had to urinate. Instead of getting up to go to the bathroom and waking her child, she asked her husband to bring her a diaper so she could urinate in that instead. Yes, really. It wasn't until I read that that it hit me how much I got out of nailing mommying perfectly and playing the martyr while doing it. Turns out I internalized the Motherhood and Apple Pie mythology more than I knew.

What if we eased up on the emotional labor? What if we let go and delegated some of the cognitive load of cake getting, stuffed animal remembering, and paperwork coordinating? I know what you're thinking, because I get sucked into that trap, too. You're thinking that if you don't do it, it won't get done right. "It's easier just to do it myself," I hear myself thinking all the time. But is it that it won't get done, or that it won't get done perfectly? And if it doesn't get done or done perfectly, is anything important really lost?

I'm not suggesting that any of us withhold love or caring or thoughtfulness from our families. Everything we do comes from a good place with the best of intentions, and much of it makes a positive difference for them. What I am suggesting, though, is that we make a distinction between what's really essential and the ways we twist ourselves into pretzels that maybe we can ease up on. When can we rely on our wisdom to know what our family members really need and when can we tune into our perfection chatter and see it as our own need for a mommy-martyr fix? When and where can we let "good enough" be exactly that?

What if we consider that while our partners may not do everything the way we would, the results—while different—may not always be lesser than? For instance, consider the results of a 2016 study conducted at the Centre for Pediatric Pain Research at the IWK Health Centre that found that though nonverbal comforting behaviors of men and women may show little difference, children who were comforted by their fathers in moments of injury or illness reported lower levels of pain intensity. If we want our partners to step up to share in this kind of emotional labor, *we need to let them do it.*

This kind of retraining is for us as much as it is for our families. What if I forgot Froggie? Shaan would have one bad night sleeping and then I guess we would have to find a Target to find a replacement. Would that suck? Yes. But maybe, just maybe, Nihal would walk past Shaan's room on our way out the door the next time we're headed out on a trip and remember to grab Froggie himself.

What if we eased up on feeling like we and we alone should do all emotional labor? What if the birthday cake came from the grocery store, or the deadline to submit the permission form for football came and went because the teenager didn't pay attention? What if we didn't rely on that hit of perfection satisfaction as proof that we're good people or parents? What if each time those of us who are moms feel the urge to nail a mommy moment flawlessly we asked ourselves if it was our inner mom-martyr voice talking?

THE (INSTAGRAM) PERFECT MOM

We've all seen them. The social media feeds of "momfluencers" who seize every opportunity to show how creative and dedicated they are as parents. Look at us bundled up in eco-friendly jackets cascading down hills on a snowy day! Here we are going on a hot-air balloon ride for our kid's birthday party! Check us out making homemade carrot raisin bread from the carrots we grew and harvested ourselves!

Dads have now gotten in on the performative parenting action, too. If you looked at my husband's Instagram feed, I swear you would think he was a single dad. Look, there is Nihal cooking dinner! Now he's taking the kids to school! Changing a diaper! These mundane parent tasks fill his feed and are met with hundreds of likes and comments about what a "cute dad" he is. It makes me crazy . . . If I posted a picture of myself taking Shaan to school, I can assure you I wouldn't be garnering praise and hand-clapping emojis.

We need to call bullshit once and for all on the performative parenting thing.

The strategy here is threefold. First, we need to see the performative parenting of other women for what it is: social media gloss. I don't say this cavalierly—we all know how hard it is to remember that social media pictures are more often than not carefully curated "moments" meant to fulfill someone's deep-seated need for perfection approval (ourselves included sometimes). This has to be a conscious untangling of what we see and what we know to be true as parents.

Second, let's collectively lay off praising dads for being "cute" when they are broadcasting themselves doing the domestic labor that we do quietly every day. I'm just as guilty of this as anyone (those societal norms run *deep*!). Just the other morning I went to get coffee at a neighborhood place and saw a young dad sitting with his kindergarten-age daughter who was eating a muffin. Instinctively I thought, "Ohh, that's so sweet." And then, as if scripted, an elderly woman walked past them and said to the girl, "What a nice daddy you have, taking you for breakfast!"

Is it sweet of that dad to take his daughter for breakfast before school on a Tuesday? Absolutely. But is it any sweeter than if a mom had taken her? And if we instinctively, like I did, think "yes," we need to do some bias rooting out.

Lastly, we need to normalize what parenting *actually* looks like. It's not all glossy perfection and we damn well know it. By all means post pictures of your family looking happy and doing wonderful things—that's straight-up joy. But check yourself to see if what you're putting out there is the whole picture of your parenting life. I'm not suggesting you post your kid's epic meltdown in the supermarket because you nixed Cap'n Crunch cereal, but how about the mismatched sneakers he wore to school that day because the morning rush to get everyone to school and work was more frantic than usual, or the lopsided cake you made from a mix for their birthday (box visible for all to see)? We free each other from the perfection trap of parenting by each showing loud and proud that more often than not, it's messy and imperfect work.

#FailureFridays

When my book *Brave, Not Perfect*, was published, I committed to broadcasting out loud on social media every Friday at least one screwup, one messy moment, one way I had shown up as less-than-perfect that week. It was my way of inviting women everywhere to climb out of the perfection trap and celebrate with me, loud and proud, the fact that we are all indelibly human.

So now I invite you to join us and let us hear your parenting failures and flops using #failurefridays. I promise you, it's so liberating. Totally spaced and left your kid waiting to be picked up from a playdate for two hours? Been there. Packed Goldfish crackers and string cheese for lunch because you had no time to make anything else? Excellent creativity. Lost your cool and told your kid to shut up? Yeah, you're not alone.

See what I mean? Liberating.

7

EDUCATE: Reimagining the Workplace

I still strongly believe that women can "have it all"
(and that men can too). I believe that we can "have it
all at the same time." But not today, not with the way
America's economy and society are currently structured.

—ANNE-MARIE SLAUGHTER

Companies are taking seriously their responsibility to step in where public policies fall short. Between January and September 2020, large corporations including Target, Citigroup, and Bank of America discussed the need for paid time off and subsidized childcare in their quarterly earnings calls.

This is a good start. But now we need to move out of talk and into action.

NINE WAYS TO MAKE THE WORKPLACE
WORK FOR WOMEN

This plan lays out nine key strategies to effect the critical changes needed to specifically support women. These strategies were developed in response to a survey of a thousand American mothers conducted jointly by the Marshall Plan for Moms and advisory and advocacy communications firm APCO Impact, and supported with research from hundreds of studies, articles, and guides, as well as insights from leading labor experts, diversity and inclusion practitioners, and visionaries shaping the future of the workplace.

Each of these strategies outlines what companies can do to change the reality for the women they employ and, at the same time, improve their bottom line. The work to repair and rebuild our workplaces for this new future requires serious commitment, but the companies that recognize their fundamental responsibility to take action will also be the ones who ultimately survive the new normal that emerges. It will also give us, as women in the workforce, strongly substantiated facts and arguments as to why these changes are so vital and insights into how we can push this agenda forward.

STRATEGY #1: GIVE WOMEN CONTROL OVER THEIR SCHEDULES

If there's a singular buzzword to emerge in our post-pandemic workforce, it's flexibility.

A survey from Grant Thornton showed that although many

American workers look forward to returning to the physical office in some capacity, an overwhelming seventy-nine percent of them also want flexibility in how, when, and where they work. When we conducted our survey for the Marshall Plan for Moms, it was no surprise that flexibility was by far the top concern of working mothers (and pretty much is for every working mother I know or have ever met).

Flexibility comes down to a singular empowering factor: having control over our schedules. Having control over our schedules means having control over our lives, and that's the first and most crucial step to getting women off the dangerous teeter-totter and onto stable ground. I think a lot about the young mom I met who told me she was fired from her job in retail because she needed to leave her shift to pick up the free laptop her son's school was giving out to enable the kids to attend school online. How many of us have felt compelled to obscure our whereabouts when we attended a parent-teacher conference during working hours, or let months or even years go by without a mammogram or colonoscopy because we literally could not leave work to make it happen?

In early 2020, many employers had no choice but to quickly implement flexible work options as stay-at-home orders and school closures collided, forcing working parents—especially moms—to adapt their work schedules to their children's needs (why doesn't work align with school hours anyway?!). On the one hand, this was a good thing, as it blew apart the notion that being physically present at a desk five days a week was the only way to work.

On the other hand, as analysis from McKinsey and others confirms that remote and hybrid working arrangements are here to stay, we need to closely watch the flex working arrangements being put in place to ensure they don't put more pressure on women to be on duty at all times in both realms. When does work begin and end if it's fluid? Enmeshing our paid work and home responsibilities is no better for our well-being than splintering and struggling to balance the two. A study published by the National Institutes of Health showed that blurred lines between work and life lead to "enhanced emotional exhaustion" and a deterioration in healthy lifestyle behaviors.

Although flexible working arrangements are considered a sexy hiring tool in our modern workplaces, availing oneself of that "perk" can have a hidden downside that can exacerbate gender inequality. Working remotely still carries a stigma, ostensibly signaling a weak commitment to one's job regardless of productivity or results, which can inhibit one's career progression. Because more women than men take advantage of flexible scheduling, they are unduly subjected to the fifty percent reduced rate of promotion linked to remote work.

The solution here for employers is to offer flexible scheduling to all employees and *encourage them all to take it*. Normalize to equalize. Pay close attention to promotion biases and prioritize output and productivity rather than facetime in the workplace.

For salaried workers, control is about *how* and *when* you work rather than *where*. A change in verbiage has helped legitimize flexibility: "Working from home," which always carried a stigma of being less committed to one's job, has been replaced with "working remotely," which reflects the one upside of the pandemic, which was a cultural acceptance of new ways of working. There are many more logistics and nuances of working remotely to be ironed out in the days to come, including how to build an environment of trust in which employers have confidence their workers are getting the job done, and in which workers who may now do their work during "non-traditional" hours feel safe to claim workday hours in which they are "off the clock." It's all about design.

Effective strategies to provide flexibility while safeguarding productivity include implementing core collaboration hours (for instance, 9 a.m. to 1 p.m.) that employees can plan around, allowing employees to set hours for asynchronous work that fits their productivity rhythms and family life, and considering flextime, a compressed workweek, shift work, part-time schedules, or job-sharing. To build an environment of trust, companies can implement what management expert and author Eve Rodsky termed "predictable flexibility." Predictable flexibility establishes a system of defined structure and communication that allows both employees and employers to plan ahead. For instance, by communicating openly about when remote work is effective and when physical team meetings are optimal, it allows employers and employees to plan ahead and establishes a culture of boundaries that makes it psychologically safe for workers to be "off the clock."

Companies who adapt to the new demands for flexibility in working hours and location will have the edge in hiring and retention in the workplace of the future. A 2020 study of ten thousand digital workers done by tech research and consulting company Gartner reported that fifty-nine percent of workers would only consider a new position or job if it allowed them to work from the location of their choice. An EY survey of sixteen thousand employees across a range of industries and job roles found that fifty-four percent would quit if their companies did not afford them some sort of flexibility in where and when they work post-pandemic.

PLAYBOOK FOR EMPLOYERS

- Offer flexible scheduling to all employees and encourage them all to take it.
- Prioritize output and productivity rather than facetime when assessing promotion candidates.
- Implement a system of "predictable flexibility" to establish a culture of trust.
- Set core collaboration hours and allow employees to set hours for asynchronous work that fits their productivity rhythms and family life.
- Consider flextime, a compressed workweek, shift work, part-time schedules, or job-sharing as flexibility options.

WHAT WOMEN CAN DO

We are not powerless to affect change in our workplaces—far from it. We need to advocate for ourselves—not by asking for a "perk" but by making a compelling case about the efficacy of flexible scheduling. Here are three ways to support your argument:

- Cite data that shows that flexibility improves productivity and engagement. For instance, according to a study commissioned in 2017 by Flex + Strategy Group, sixty percent of workers with work flexibility reported feeling "more productive and engaged." Only four percent said they are less so. In a study of ten thousand digital workers done by tech research and consulting company Gartner, forty-three percent of workers reported that flexibility in working hours increased their productivity.
- Clarify that flexibility can be compatible with structure. Instead of saying "I want to work remotely a few days a week," propose a specific schedule (for instance, "I want to work remotely on Mondays and Wednesdays" or "I'll log off at 4 p.m. and finish my work in the evenings between 7 to 9 p.m." Explain how and when you'll communicate your progress and how you'll collaborate on remote workdays (e.g., "I'll respond promptly to instant messages, document all my progress, and send an email round-up each week").

- Point to large corporations who are effectively instituting these changes. In 2018, Walmart, the United States' largest private employer, introduced a new system for associates that allowed them to establish more fixed shifts and worker-controlled scheduling options. Associates were given the ability to view their schedules on an app, as well as swap shifts and pick up unfilled shifts if they wanted. For consistency, Walmart implemented a method called "core hours," in which an associate works the same weekly shifts for at least thirteen weeks, allowing the associate the stability to plan their life around their work schedule.

STRATEGY #2: SUPPORT WOMEN WITH CHILDCARE

"Before the pandemic, I used to go into a panic whenever I woke up to an email from my kids' school saying they were closed for a snow day," said Marianna, a mother of three kids under the age of nine. "I'd get such a pit in my stomach knowing that my entire workday would be lost and that my boss—who has no kids and likes to call mine 'rug rats'—would definitely not understand. I laugh about that now because 2020 was like the longest snow day from hell."

If the pandemic showed us anything, it's that the availability of childcare dictates women's ability to work—and, in the longer term, to stay in the workforce at all. When care centers and schools closed, forcing millions of women to leave the workforce because they relied on those resources—or employed caregivers who in turn relied on these resources for their own children—it became crystal clear that access to childcare is a key component to the future of work. Bottom line: Without affordable, reliable, quality childcare, *we cannot work*. Our livelihood literally depends on this.

America has faced a childcare crisis for years. The supply is way below the demand, and many lower-income families either live in areas outside of major cities that are childcare deserts or barely scrape together tuition. According to the Institute of Child, Youth and Family Policy at Brandeis University, in 2018, childcare was unaffordable for sixty-three percent of full-time working parents. But parents who earn a decent income are not guaranteed to find a viable childcare solution, either. Though the Department of Health and Human Services recommends that families spend no more than seven percent of their income on childcare, couples earning the national median income of $87,757 spend an estimated 10.6 percent on childcare (for one child . . . costs increase exponentially for additional children). Single parents—of which this country has the highest percentage in the world—may spend up to thirty-seven percent.

In the wake of the pandemic, agencies who place in-home nannies and babysitters are reporting a nationwide shortage of private caregivers resulting in skyrocketing premiums for these roles that many families simply cannot afford to pay. A publicist I know who is married to a college professor lamented, "I earn a good living, but honestly, at this point I am working just to pay for the babysitter. My wife and I sit around every night and wonder if it's really worth it . . . if one of us should just stay home with our kids instead and make some cuts."

That is a depressing choice. At the same time, many families in America do not have the luxury of even considering this option, as the financial stability of their family unit depends on the dual income of both parents and there are no viable cuts they can make. That reality is even more stark for single parents who are the sole support system for the family. In those instances, being unable to pay for childcare so both parents can work goes from being a troubling burden to a serious crisis.

Less than half of U.S. employers gave childcare assistance during the pandemic, though mainly through remote working and flexible scheduling options. Only one percent provided direct support in the form of backup childcare or on-site facilities. As advocacy group TIME'S UP reported, while the former was helpful (somewhat) during the long months of lockdown, if companies want to bring women back into the workforce, this direct support isn't just a perk that's "nice to have." It's a must.

PLAYBOOK FOR EMPLOYERS

Every working parent needs a childcare arrangement that fits their unique family situation and working schedule, so options are key. Here is the spectrum of solutions some companies are already offering to enable families to tailor solutions that work for them:

- Offer employees access to resources that help find caregivers and babysitters in your area. Best Buy, Starbucks, and CarGurus give their employees access to Care.com, a resource to find babysitters and other caregivers. Fidelity Investments provides a concierge for parents to help them find availability in local daycare centers.
- Provide free or subsidized on-site care. Mercedes Benz, Georgia Pacific, Aflac, Cerner, Goldman Sachs, Johnson & Johnson, and many other large corporations have recognized this pressing need and invested in on-site facilities.
- Provide free or subsidized care at a childcare center or in-home. Facebook provides an annual childcare subsidy of $3,000 and Bank of America reimburses eligible employees up to $275 per month for childcare. Citibank provides its employees with subsidies for external childcare and eldercare.
- Provide free or subsidized backup care. Amazon, Apple, and General Motors have partnered with Bright Horizons Family Solutions to provide backup care for their employees. Facebook subsidizes ten days per year of backup care and Bank of America provides fifty.
- Negotiate discounts on behalf of your employees with local childcare centers.
- Offer flexible spending accounts so parents can pay for childcare with pre-tax dollars. As of 2018, sixty-seven percent of companies offered dependent care FSAs.

WHAT WOMEN CAN DO

- Band together to advocate. As women in a workplace, you have more power together than you do alone.
- Be specific in your ask. Educate yourselves on the variety of caregiving options in your area or that other companies comparable to yours are implementing and propose tangible options to your employer from the list above. Good resources to explore include www.childcare.gov and www.care.com.
- Educate your employer on the cost of *not* subsidizing childcare. If parents do not have childcare, they cannot work, which leads to absences and greater employee turnover. According to Gallup, the cost of replacing an individual employee is anywhere from one-half to two times an employee's annual salary—and, as Gallup qualify, this is a conservative estimate.

STRATEGY #3: OWN YOUR ROLE IN SHAPING GENDER DYNAMICS AT HOME

What do employers have to do with perpetuating gendered dynamics in the home? Far more than you might think.

Stay with me here and I'll show you how this plays out.

In a relationship between heterosexual parents, women on average do fifty percent more of the caregiving. Women on average also spend two hours more per day doing housework than their male counterparts. There are a variety of theories as to why this is so (and no, the idea that men are "dirt blind" is not one of them; that theory thankfully has been debunked), but the most salient is that because labor in the home, which encompasses cleaning and taking care of children or elderly family members, is not valued in our society to the same degree as paid labor and is thus deemed as unattractive and unworthy work. Cooking is an interesting chore to look at here, because when it's done outside the home in a professional capacity, it's a highly competitive, respected field in which men dominate to the tune of occupying a little over three-fourths of the coveted professional chef positions in this country. When it's done *inside* the home of married or cohabitating parents, however, a whopping eighty percent of mothers say they are the ones who most often prepare the meals.

"The closer you are to a diaper in your work, the less valued you are and the less pay you get—on both ends of the age distribution, whether it's caring for infants or the dying. You face obstacles in terms of every important resource you need to thrive. And that's why it's wrong. It's like the decline of Roman civilization—we're done if we can't take care of the most needy."

—PROFESSOR STEWART FRIEDMAN,
WHARTON WORK/LIFE INTEGRATION PROJECT
AT THE UNIVERSITY OF PENNSYLVANIA

None of this is meant to point an accusatory finger at men. I think it's safe to say that the majority of men don't consciously form the thought, "I'm not the one who should wash the sheets or stay home when our kid has strep throat because I am a man, and my time is more valuable." But societal norms have a powerful way of shaping our psyches. We exist in a society in which ninety percent of the employees in the childcare industry are women. According to the U.S. Census Bureau, 88.6 percent of housekeepers are women and seventy-three percent are people of color. That sends a clear message about who in our culture is expected to fulfill those roles. The belief that "care work is women's work" is pretty deeply ingrained—so much so that many men during the pandemic preferred to remain unemployed than step into the plethora of those jobs that came available, which is why we are still facing such a dearth of workers in those industries.

And here's where the typical workplace in America comes into play: Less than half of all companies offer paid paternity leave, likely due in no small part to the societal expectation of who should be caring for newborns and the value—or, more accurately, non-value—we place on work in the home. Kudos to the companies like Netflix, Microsoft, Walmart, eBay, and Deloitte who are leading the charge on gender-neutral parental leave, as well as the companies who are offering "parental bonding leave" and "secondary caregiver leave" for LGBTQ and adoptive parents. This is a good start, but to truly change the tide and make a powerful statement about the value of home labor and caregiving, companies need to go beyond offering paid parental leave. They need to *build a culture that encourages dads to take it without professional consequences.*

This has two layers. First, it means eradicating the outdated macho bullshit propagated by leaders like Joe Lonsdale, cofounder of Palantir Technologies Inc., who tweeted in response to U.S. transportation secretary Pete Buttigieg taking time off to care for his newborns that men who take family leave are "losers." Lonsdale isn't alone in this. When New York Mets second baseman Daniel Murphy missed opening day in 2014 because he was on paternity leave, radio host Mike Francesa chided, "You're a major league baseball player—you can hire a nurse to take care of the baby if your wife needs help."

Second, it means paying up by incentivizing, even mandating, family leave for new fathers and partners of birthing mothers and tying performance reviews, pay, and promotion considerations to it. The U.S. Department of Labor states that the vast majority of fathers take some time off after their children are born, but the majority of them take less than ten days away from the job. It's not hard to connect the dots to ascertain why. If you are a company that touts that you offer a generous paid leave policy, unless you also show that the men at your firm take full advantage of the policy, you don't get bragging rights.

"These are not women's issues; they are family issues. The approach must be de-gendered, otherwise it may move us all back."

—BRAD HARRINGTON, EXECUTIVE DIRECTOR AND

RESEARCH PROFESSOR, CENTER FOR WORK AND FAMILY,

CARROLL SCHOOL OF MANAGEMENT AT BOSTON COLLEGE

The benefits of nurturing a company culture that encourages family leave are compelling. Research shows that family leave produces happier, more productive working dads. A McKinsey study reported that fathers who took paid leave feel more motivated and remain more committed to their employers, which we can deduce leads to less turnover. They also became more productive and prioritized their time better— again, better work practices lead to better bottom lines. Paid gender-neutral leave allows for a more even distribution of the "invisible labor" of raising children and running a household; this leveling of the playing field can in turn help women remain in the workforce and reverse the alarming trend triggered by the pandemic.

There are also downstream benefits of men taking parental leave that help reshape the dynamics at home. When we as a culture normalize gender-neutral parental leave as opposed to just maternity leave, we begin to make the tectonic shift in how we value caregiving. A McKinsey & Company report released in March 2021 reported on the positive impact paternity leave (and, more crucially, fathers' shared involvement in the first few months of a child's life) has on families, which includes strengthening partnerships and forging lifelong bonds with children, mitigating postpartum depression in mothers, and setting a foundation for an equal and fair distribution of household responsibilities.

> *"Fathers taking parental leave helps not just children but moms, too, by changing who changes the diapers and the whole culture around work and family."*
> —TOM PEREZ, FORMER U.S. SECRETARY OF LABOR

PLAYBOOK FOR EMPLOYERS

- Establish a generous paid parental leave policy that offers the same benefits to all new parents—biological or adoptive, primary or secondary caregiver.
- Encourage leaders in your organization to set an example by taking full paternity leave, to remove the social stigma around caregiving. By way of example, Facebook CEO Mark Zuckerberg took two months off when his children were born to help create a new norm within his company culture.
- Be out front with your support for creating an equal dynamic in the home. In a press release announcing its expanded gender-neutral parental leave policy,

food-products corporation Danone North America (parent company of Dannon, Evian, and more) expressly stated that the intent of the policy was to recognize that ". . . parenting is a shared responsibility between caregivers. It is intended to create a more equitable workplace and in doing so, challenge traditional assumptions on caregiving and help advance equality for all."

WHAT WOMEN CAN DO

While I vowed not to veer into "ways to fix our partners," the reality here is that less than half of men who are given paid parental leave take full advantage of all the time offered to them. If your partner is in that majority, here are some proven facts that might help shift his perspective:

- Women whose partners took paternity leave make more money in the long run. A study out of Sweden showed that a woman's income rose 6.7 percent for every month that her partner took leave.
- Breastfeeding is boosted by a partner's presence. A 2014 study done by the National Academy of Sciences found that having their partner at home raises the levels of prolactin and oxytocin in new mothers, the hormones responsible for stimulating breastmilk.
- Another study found that when dads tune in regularly to their newborns' cries, it creates neural pathways in

the father's brain related to social perception, increasing his ability to forge and maintain relationships. (Not a bad skill to have in the workplace once he goes back.)

- A study of four OECD (Organisation for Economic Co-operation and Development) countries, including the United States, revealed that longer paternity leaves are associated with higher cognitive test scores and fewer behavior problems in children.

- Fathers who take paternity leave report higher satisfaction with parenting and enjoy stronger bonds over time with their children.

STRATEGY #4: GIVE PARENTS PAID TIME OFF FOR ILLNESS

When the highly capable Gloria decided to have a baby on her own at age thirty-six, she was absolutely certain (like most women I know, yours truly included) that she would be able to neatly fit parenting into her life as an investor relations manager at a large corporation. She was, after all, the self-proclaimed "Time Management Queen" who was known as being ultra-efficient. If she just tightly managed the scheduling and delegated, everything would run like clockwork . . . right? Her meticulously constructed plan was to take precisely ten weeks of maternity leave (no need for the full twelve!), returning to work online for a few hours each afternoon while a babysitter came, then once she went back to the office the babysitter would handle all the childcare during the workdays up through bath time when she would return to put the baby to bed.

"Oh, please," Gloria laughed, rolling her eyes. "For the first few months of her life, Sophie had colic and would not stop screaming, so I had three babysitters quit on me until I found one that stayed. Each time I lost about three or four days of work. When the baby was about nine months old, my babysitter called me frantically the morning of our quarterly earnings call—which let's just say is my company's version of the Super Bowl—because Sophie had rolled off the changing table. I had to rush home to take her to the hospital and dialed into the call from a supply closet in the E.R. Let's just say my CEO was not very happy with me." The Time Management Queen was officially dethroned when Sophie started preschool. "I swear that kid was ground zero for lice," Gloria joked, grimacing. "*Three times* that first year I got the call from the school nurse that I had to come pick her up right away. Then she and I would have to stay home for a minimum of three days, and believe me, no babysitter will come within twenty feet of a kid with head lice."

Now forty-two with a six-year-old (who yes, still somehow gets lice yearly), Gloria knows all too well the sobering reality of parenting: Kids are not robots, and neither they nor the countless runny noses, ear infections, stomach flus, lice or chicken pox outbreaks, or broken bones (or, after puberty, broken hearts) give a hoot about your quarterly earnings call. They are little humans, with human needs and human illnesses that rarely, if ever, occur when you conveniently have an opening in your schedule.

Gloria is fortunate to work in a high-paying industry that offers up to ten days of paid sick leave per year, yet for millions in this country, paid time off for illness or caregiving is a "perk" they simply don't have. While the Family and Medical Leave Act of 1993 allows for job-protected leave, it is unpaid. The workers most likely to be impacted by this are women, who are ten times more likely than men to take time off to stay home with their sick child and five times more likely to be the one taking a sick child to the doctor. Women also fill as much as eighty-one percent of caregiving roles for elderly parents at home. But women should not have to choose between their health or the health of their families and a paycheck.

It would not be an overstatement to say that during the pandemic, when illness was the primary concern, the toll of having to make such a choice was devastating for women's mental health—not to mention their bank accounts. The 2021 "Women in the Workplace" report from McKinsey & Company and LeanIn.Org chronicles an alarming spike in the burnout rate of women, with forty-two percent reporting feeling pushed to the brink "often" or "almost always," and the gap between the burnout rates of women and men has nearly doubled.

In the survey we conducted with APCO of one thousand working women, ninety-two percent of women ranked paid sick leave as critical, not only for themselves, but for their children. This form of leave is a given in countries like Australia,

Sweden, and Germany—and it is time for it to be instituted by companies here in the United States. Working women need to be able to care for their families and for themselves without putting their livelihood at risk.

PLAYBOOK FOR EMPLOYERS

Let parents take the time to care for themselves and their families. To support family well-being and create stronger workplaces in the process:

- Allow employees to accrue sick days as they work. According to the Bureau of Labor Statistics, employees in most companies earn between five and nine sick days per year.
- Provide paid, job-protected leave for parents to care for a sick child at home.
- Build a culture in your workplace that encourages employees to avail themselves of paid sick leave policies.
- Encourage leaders in your organization to take time off to attend to sick children as needed—*without hiding that they are doing so.* At Girls Who Code, we hold each other accountable to putting family first; that means missing a board meeting if your little one is sick.
- To support the mental and physical health of employees, communicate clearly to employees that those on sick or

caregiving leave are not required nor expected to be "on the clock." A small business owner I know mandates that anyone in his company who is out on sick leave put an automated "away from email" notice in effect to reinforce this policy—both for the sick worker so they don't feel pressure to have to check their emails and so others can see the policy in action.

• Provide leeway and resources for your employees who have additional caregiving needs. McKinsey & Company, for instance, provides parents of kids with special needs (including babies born prematurely) with twenty extra paid days of parental leave as well as access to an affinity network and guidance from firm-contracted doctors.

WHAT WOMEN CAN DO

To support your argument for paid sick leave, point out the economic upside of guaranteed paid sick leave for your employer. Paid time off reduces absenteeism, but it also reduces the risk of contagion that would lead to far greater absences. Research has shown that employees who do not have paid sick leave are more likely to go to work while sick and spread contagious diseases. In the post-COVID era, the case for encouraging employees to stay home when they or a family member is sick is a pretty easy one to make.

STRATEGY #5: ROOT OUT THE MOTHERHOOD PENALTY

Anti-mom bias is one of the biggest open secrets in the workplace. Every woman who has children has either experienced it or knows someone who has. Seiko, for instance, was a top earner in a real estate agency when she became pregnant with her first child. In a "you've got to be kidding me" plot point, she actually overheard two senior agents discussing her news while they were in the elevator, unaware that Seiko was in the back of the crowded car. One of the senior agents, an older woman with no children, said something to the effect of, "So much for those earnings after she has the kid . . . if she's even coming back."

A plethora of research shows that working moms are seen as less reliable, less committed, and less competent, regardless of how strong their performance record was before. There is no question that mothers are more likely to be judged for their caregiving responsibilities. Women on a broad scale encounter hostility or become "mommy-tracked" when they become pregnant, take parental leave, or avail themselves of a flexible work schedule. One study confirmed that visibly pregnant women managers are viewed as less dependable and less committed to their jobs than their non-pregnant counterparts; another showed that evaluators rated a consultant with children as "less competent" than one without.

Big shocker: The motherhood penalty shows up in hiring practices as well. In a 2007 landmark study, researchers from

Cornell University sent out fictitious applications to employers, some that made reference to the applicant having children and some not. The applicants whose information made no reference to children were twice as likely to be asked to come in for an interview.

We're all well familiar by now with the concept of women hitting the glass ceiling, but working moms are confronted with another gender bias known as the "maternal wall." Just like it sounds, this wall appears in front of women right at the point that they have children. The maternal wall bias shows up in ways obvious and subtle, from microaggressions to poor performance evaluations to being passed over for jobs, assignments, or promotions. McKinsey notes that in 2021 women of color were particularly prone to being subjected to disrespectful or "othering" behaviors like these, creating a double whammy bias. Some women are involuntarily nudged into lower-visibility, lower-reward positions, a phenomenon known as "downshifting."

> "Biases are not necessarily ones you can call out, but you feel them within the organization. Employers equate reliability with being in the workforce uninterruptedly. There is this idea that a woman who leaves to have a child isn't reliable."
>
> —ALEJANDRA CASTILLO, FORMER CEO, YMCA

This bias goes hand in hand with its cousin phenomenon, known as "the motherhood penalty." Coined by sociologists Dr. Michelle Budig and Dr. Paula England, the motherhood penalty is specifically economic and refers to the wage penalties associated with becoming and being a mother. That penalty, which costs women an average of fifteen percent of income per child, accounts for much of the gender pay gap. For Black and Native American women, the motherhood wage penalty increases to twenty percent; Latinas face an eighteen percent penalty and Asian women thirteen percent. While fathers experience no wage penalties, one study shows the pay gap between childless women and mothers under age thirty-five is greater than the pay gap between men and women.

It is estimated that family-forward public policies along the ones currently under debate in Congress would decrease the motherhood penalty by one-third. Until such time that the full breadth of sweeping policy changes we need go into effect, it's up to companies to step up and root out this under-addressed aspect of gender bias to put mothers on equal footing.

PLAYBOOK FOR EMPLOYERS

- Challenge unconscious biases against women by raising awareness of the stereotypes and stigmas that mothers face. Require all employees to do unconscious bias training and encourage leaders to speak out against these biases.

- Check for bias in the allocation of assignments and encourage working mothers to take on highly valued roles.
- Ensure that evaluations focus more on ability and productivity than on physical time spent at work, and that they reward leadership qualities that moms are more likely to possess, like fostering team building.
- Track whether women are penalized for flexible schedules or part-time work.
- Evaluate on an ongoing basis pay of mothers and fathers doing equal work and rectify any discrepancies.
- Assess algorithms in hiring software that disqualify moms who have taken career breaks for caregiving.
- Implement leadership development programs that target moms.

WHAT WOMEN CAN DO

The way we destigmatize working motherhood is to bring it out of the shadows and *stop hiding*!

Here is our chance to "parent loudly." A good example of parenting loudly on a big stage is when the women leaders of Rent the Runway brought their kids to the NASDAQ the day their company went public. I was so inspired by this that when, as the Godmother of Celebrity Cruises, I christened their new ship the *Celebrity Apex* in front of a slew of corporate and media representatives, I brought my two-year-old son with me to do the honors. (I have to say he looked dashing in his tuxedo.)

But you don't need to host a public event with your kid on your hip to parent loudly. You can share some good news about your kid, say straight out that you won't be at the afternoon meeting because it's your son's fifth birthday, or refuse to hide that you are taking a few days off to visit potential colleges with your high school senior. If I could do my early years all over again, I'd go back to the buttoned-up law firm I worked for and post pictures of my niece Maya up at my desk as a way to claim my right to be both a worker *and* a parental figure to someone I love.

I don't say any of this lightly. I know boldness in these circumstances takes bravery—bravery to step outside the comfort zone of the norm, bravery to show up as less than perfect (i.e., the "ideal worker" who is unencumbered), bravery to take a stand for your emotional rights as a mother. But I also know from years of research and writing about women and bravery that it is a skill that we can absolutely cultivate.

STRATEGY #6: DON'T RUSH NEW MOTHERS BACK TO WORK BEFORE THEY ARE READY

With the exception of Papua New Guinea, the United States is the only country in the world that has no national policy guaranteeing leave for new mothers. New mothers in Denmark receive eighteen weeks of fully paid leave, including four prior to birth. Sweden also gives new mothers eighteen weeks of fully paid leave, as well as up to 480 days of leave at eighty percent of their pay. Serbian mothers are entitled to up to twenty weeks of paid leave. We'll discuss in the next chapter the government's responsibility to amend this stupefying lack—and *fast*—but in the meantime, it is up to employers to step up and make new motherhood a compensated priority.

Accounting firms are leading the charge on mom-friendly policies. PricewaterhouseCoopers, for instance, gives birthing mothers sixteen weeks of paid leave and eight weeks for adoptive or foster parents. KPMG offers seventeen weeks of paid leave for new mothers and four weeks for new fathers, and Deloitte gives up to sixteen weeks of paid time off to bond with a child after birth or adoption. It's not surprising that these firms repeatedly earn top spots on lists like the Top Companies for Executive Women, *Working Mother*'s 100 Best Companies, and others.

Besides subsidizing gender-neutral parental leave, companies need to *stop rushing new mothers back to work before they are ready*. Childbirth is no walk in the park, and moms need time to recover as well as time to bond with their new babies. The sick but true joke about what the world would be like if men gave birth has been told so many times in so many ways, but this Instagram post from a woman I follow was probably my favorite: "At 4 weeks postpartum I was sleeping 3 'nonconsecutive' hours a night; breastfeeding every 2 hours for at least 30 minutes a session, so about 6 hours a day; and bleeding through everything I wore. If men did this, the whole fucking world would be structured around parental leave."

Again and again, research shows us that parents having

time at home to care for their newborns has a profound impact on health and well-being. Each week a mother stays home with her newborn reduces the odds of postpartum depression—a serious and dangerous condition that afflicts one in seven women who give birth and around nine hundred thousand women annually, taking into account those who miscarry or have a stillbirth. Paid leave is also associated with reduced infant mortality rate; researchers estimate that providing twelve weeks of paid, job-protected leave would result in six hundred fewer infant deaths per year.

PLAYBOOK FOR EMPLOYERS

- Give mothers the time they need to be with their babies and recover from childbirth and *do not rush them to come back before they are ready.*
- Make this an out-loud policy within your organization so new mothers are not subjected to microaggressions or subtle pressures.
- Offer paid maternity leave that aligns with the OECD standards, which is a minimum of twelve weeks.

WHAT WOMEN CAN DO

Educate your employer about the benefits of generous paid leave for their bottom line. Here are just a few of the studies showing that generous, unrushed paid leave pays off:

- The National Partnership for Women & Families attests that paid leave reduces employee turnover; some estimates put the cost of employee turnover as high as one-fifth of an employee's annual salary.
- A study out of Rutgers showed that women who take paid parental leave are ninety-three percent more likely to still be in the workforce nine to twelve months later than women who don't.
- Productivity and hiring are also positively impacted. An EY survey found that eighty percent of companies with paid parental leave reported higher employee morale and seventy percent reported a boost in productivity. A Deloitte survey showed that more than three-fourths of workers could be more inclined toward employers who offer paid leave.
- Paid leave gives small businesses an edge over their larger competitors. A study published in the *Harvard Business Review* that surveyed companies in California found that those with fewer than a hundred employees reported greater positive outcomes in profitability, productivity, turnover, and morale than those with one hundred or more.

STRATEGY #7: IMPLEMENT STRONG REENTRY STRATEGIES

If women are the ones who do the gestating and birthing (which we are by biological design) and also the ones who are more likely to stay home to raise kids either by necessity or choice (which—at least for now—we do by societal default), then we need the freedom, resources, and support to be able to move in and out of the workforce without penalty. Period. Full stop.

Regardless of whether a woman took three months after becoming a new mom or three years off to raise young children, returning to work can be a challenging transition. When moms are ready to come back to work, strong re-onboarding programs are critical to ensure the obstacles of the maternal wall and burnout don't send them heading right back out the door.

> *"The holy grail should be that when someone goes to an employer to say that they're having a child the reaction is, 'Awesome—you're about to become a better employee because I will support the hell out of you on your journey and you will grow.'"*
>
> —AMY HENDERSON, CO-LEADER,
> FAMTECH FOUNDERS COLLABORATION

Becoming a mother is a major life transition, especially the first time around. We already know the pressures of juggling childcare responsibilities with work obligations, so it is essential that direct managers demonstrate empathy and establish strong and open lines of communication to ensure mothers are staying afloat. Most retention rates for new mothers don't happen in the immediate; rather, it is twelve to eighteen months later that women drop out, likely due in no small part to a lack of in-house support.

The pandemic ushered in a huge wave of women who stepped away from the workforce to care for children. With the shortage of workers plaguing the country, employers are eager to bring women back. In early 2021, Amazon announced an expansion of its "returnship" program, committing to bring back at least one thousand women to its workforce. A prominent career reentry consulting firm estimates that as many as eighty Fortune 500 companies will offer returnships by 2026. According to Women Back to Work, an employment resource for women seeking to return to the labor force after a gap, benefits to companies of establishing returnships include access to an untapped talent pool and a pipeline of female talent, highly motivated employees, and a boost to the company reputation as a progressive and positive place to work.

PLAYBOOK FOR EMPLOYERS

- Build returnship programs to give women a structured and supported reentry plan.
- Create a tailored coaching program for new mothers and other women returning to the workplace that includes regular manager and human resources check-ins to discuss work-life issues. At Danone, every new parent has a one-on-one interview with their line manager and

human resources (HR) to discuss and agree on how the company can support their reintegration back into the workplace.

- Offer a flexible schedule, part-time work, or job-sharing to allow new mothers to transition back to full time while adjusting to childcare responsibilities.

- Provide dignified basic support that new moms need upon returning to work, like well-equipped, comfortable lactation rooms and milk delivery services for mothers on business travel.

- Provide resources and support for managers. Teach managers to avoid making assumptions around new mothers' capacities and to communicate directly with new moms about their career aspirations.

- Track data on new mothers and their engagement, re-tention, and promotion rates to ensure "mommy-track-ing" is not taking hold.

- Create a non-gendered parents' resource forum within your organization for parents to connect. Recruitment should target both mothers and fathers to normalize parenting as a shared responsibility across gender lines. Citigroup, for instance, created an employee group called "Families Matter," to enable working parents to connect with other parents who can help with questions and challenges.

- Establish a resource concierge or provide access to re-sources that new parents need. eBay, for instance, offers formal parenting coaching to its employees via Cleo, an online family support platform.

- Demonstrate your commitment to fostering the careers of mothers by actively recruiting women who are expecting or have children. As a single mother, Stephanie Synclair initiated a drive to hire other single mothers when she launched La Rue 1680, a luxury-tea start-up.

WHAT WOMEN CAN DO

- If you have taken some time away from the workforce and are looking to go back, start by checking out some of the excellent resources available such as: https://www.womenbacktowork.org/, https://www.ellevatenetwork.com/, and https://themomproject.com/.
- If you already are employed, pitch a returnship program to be instituted within your company. Remember, we need to advocate for one another! The statistics and benefits explained above will go a long way in supporting your argument.
- If your company already has a returnship program, offer to mentor one or more of the women in the program.

STRATEGY #8: PRIORITIZE WOMEN'S MENTAL HEALTH

In the fall of 2021, the *Harvard Business Review* ran an article titled "It's a New Era for Mental Health at Work." Now THAT is a work truism we can and should all lean into.

Stress in the workplace is no joke. The American Psychiatric Association estimates that excessive work stress is linked to a staggering one hundred twenty million deaths per year; $48 billion each year is spent on health issues related directly to high demands and pressure at work. Besides the high rates of absenteeism and turnover created by burnout, overwhelming evidence shows that people who suffer from depression and/or anxiety triggered by stress are more susceptible to substance abuse, heart disease, cancer, hypertension, diabetes, and a range of other illnesses, all of which increase healthcare costs.

American women in the workforce passed "stressed" ages ago and have rounded the corner into crisis territory. Even pre-pandemic, women reported higher levels of work-related stress compared to their male colleagues shaped by double standards, gender discrimination, and the unrelenting demands of juggling work and home responsibilities. These stresses were compounded mightily for working mothers during the pandemic, who, as McKinsey reported, were three times as likely as fathers to take on the increased load of caregiving and housework. As a result, millions of mothers watched helplessly as their job security went up in smoke—and their dreams and ambitions along with it.

The Conference Board reports that sixty-one percent of workers who left the workforce, particularly women and millennials, point to stress and burnout as their main concern in returning. If employers do not move quickly to take strong, proactive measures to secure and stabilize the mental health of their workers, they risk losing even more women from their ranks—both the ones they have now and the ones they hope to hire in the future—along with the diversity and innovation capital they bring to the table.

All the strategies outlined above will positively impact women's mental health, from removing the extreme stresses around securing childcare to liberating women from having to hide their motherhood (current or future desired), providing them with paid sick and parental leave so they never again have to choose between their well-being or the well-being of their family and a paycheck, and creating a workplace culture that champions parents and roots out the motherhood penalty in all its insidious forms. But employers also need to proactively and preemptively head off the burnout. According to data collected by health start-up Maven, companies who take steps to reduce worker burnout by directly addressing the causes see a twentyfold increase in employees' likelihood to stay.

One way is by eradicating the "always on" culture that slowly crept in before the pandemic and then, all at once, became the norm. Beyond parental and sick leave, working mothers must be given—*and must be encouraged to take*—time off to rest, whether at the end of the workday, on weekends, or on paid time off for vacations. Additionally, employers must respect women's "off-duty time." Not by paying lip service, but by instituting real policies in the workplace, both official and cultural. I recently received an email from a prominent business leader and the permanent tagline on her signoff said, "I do not expect a response to my email outside your normal working hours." Brilliant.

Below are more sound strategies employers can institute to prioritize the mental health of women in their workplaces.

Calling All Leaders

In a memo to employees during the pandemic, Citigroup CEO Jane Fraser declared Fridays videoconferencing-free days as a way to encourage workers to establish healthier work-life boundaries. "The blurring of lines between home and work and the relentlessness of the pandemic workday have taken a toll on our well-being," she wrote. "It's simply not sustainable . . . we need to reset some of our working practices."

That's the kind of leadership we need to continue in our post-pandemic reality.

PLAYBOOK FOR EMPLOYERS

- Implement paid time off policies that align with OECD averages. Most countries allow for approximately thirty to thirty-five days of paid leave annually, including public holidays.
- Establish an annual time-off minimum to encourage employees to use their vacation days. Many companies

require their employees to take five consecutive days at least once a year to ensure they unplug and recharge.

- Lead by example. Managers and senior leaders should take vacation time to promote a culture in which that is accepted and expected.

- Respect your workers' private time in the evenings and on weekends and vacation time. Make your time-off boundaries a clearly stated company policy and provide training for managers to cement this practice in place.

- Along with performance reviews, conduct regular wellness reviews with each employee. Additionally, consider hiring a wellness coordinator that employees can consult with as needed.

- Train managers to check in with employees regularly to discuss their levels of stress and watch for signs of burnout, which include an obvious loss of motivation and productivity, detachment, increased absenteeism, visible fatigue, or an increase in cynicism or pessimism.

- Establish on-site or access to health and wellness programs. A survey of 256 companies by the National Alliance of Healthcare Purchaser Coalitions found that more than half are providing such programs for their employees in the wake of the pandemic.

- Cover or subsidize costs for mental health providers. PricewaterhouseCoopers will pay for up to six therapy sessions annually and Starbucks offers associates up to twenty counseling sessions per year.

- Offer resources such as resilience and stress training programs, meditation classes, and discounted access to wellness apps. Target provides employees access to Daylight, an app to help users navigate stress, and Sleepio, an app to help improve sleep. PricewaterhouseCoopers offers well-being coaching sessions with a professional coach to help employees navigate stress.

- Emphasize and support physical health and nutrition. Negotiate discounts at local fitness centers and provide free or subsidized lunch from healthy take-out restaurants nearby.

WHAT WOMEN CAN DO

- Make your basic wellness needs non-negotiable. Step away from work to go to the doctor when you need to. Leave work at a reasonable time to get to the gym. Take your vacation days (for real). If you need backup, remind your employer that the World Health Organization reported that workplaces that promote and support mental health see increased productivity and economic gains.

- State your boundaries out loud, *without apologizing.* I worked once with an editor who, when I suggested an after-work drink time for our meeting (this was before I had kids), responded very kindly but firmly, "I don't do work meetings after 5 p.m." I thought that was *fantastic*.

- Stick to your personal commitments. If it's the night of your kid's school play, no, you cannot stay late. If you are working toward not responding to emails over the weekend, then *don't respond to emails*. This is as much about our own willpower as it is resetting others' expectations.

- Let go of the "unpaid labor" you take on at work. Do you really need to *always* be the one who plans every office birthday celebration, coordinates the office book club, or takes time away from her work to counsel colleagues who are having a rough day?

- Reduce the unhealthy stress of hiding your motherhood at work. Lead by example and normalize being a strong, capable woman in the workforce who is also raising the next generation. Tell them you like to drop your kid off at school in the morning, so you can't be at meetings until 9:30. And do this about things you *want* to do with your kids, not just the things you *have* to do. This sends the signal that you value your home life as much as your work life and they should, too.

- Keep a watchful eye for signs of burnout. These most often include exhaustion, cynicism, and lack of productivity. If you sense you are veering into burnout territory, let your employer know so you can talk through ways to mitigate the stressors. The stigma around it is greatly lessening as the mental health of workers is becoming an increased priority for business leaders. Many companies now are not only aware of burnout but, as outlined above, are investing in resources to help support their employees suffering from mental health strains.

STRATEGY #9: ADVOCATE FOR MOTHERS PUBLICLY

As employers, we need you to advocate for us—*loudly*. Advocacy is about standing up for what is right, and what's right here is to stand up for your employees who identify as moms to enable them to thrive as employees. If you want the eighty-six million women who are mothers at some point in their lifetime to show up and work for you, you need to show up and work for us.

PLAYBOOK FOR EMPLOYERS

- Use your leverage and push policymakers to support mom-friendly public policies. These include the expansion of child tax credits or subsidies, increased limits on flex-spending accounts that can be used for childcare, greater access to universal preschool, free or subsidized afterschool-care programs, and revisions to the tax system to eliminate penalties for dual-income households.
- Join the Care Economy Business Council, a large coalition of corporations and businesses including JPMorgan Chase, Google, and Spotify that are partnering with women's advocacy group TIME'S UP to change the

narrative around caregiving and advocate for public policies to address the childcare crisis.

- Pledge publicly your stated commitment to hiring mothers. Accenture, for instance, committed to hiring 150 moms in top roles and is working with the Mom Project, a marketplace that connects professional women with companies, to source candidates.
- Push the pro-business lobby groups you are part of to support policies that are pro-family and pro–working moms. In the past, many pro-business lobby groups were against policies like paid leave. That's changing, but not fast enough.

8

REVISE: Shifting the Narrative in Our Culture

For me, being a mother made me a better professional, because coming home every night to my girls reminded me what I was working for. And being a professional made me a better mother, because by pursuing my dreams, I was modeling for my girls how to pursue their dreams.

—MICHELLE OBAMA

"Yes, but *how* is this all going to happen?"

That's what Jackie, a friend of mine, asked me over dinner when I told her about how we were going to revolutionize the future of work for women by changing the balance and value of invisible, unpaid labor we do at home.

At first, I was a little annoyed and thought ever-so-briefly about draining the last of my wine and putting a quick end to our evening. What did she mean, *how* was it going to happen? We were going to fight like hell to put into law the public policies that would support working mothers and compensate them for the unpaid labor that was effectively the backbone of our economy. Employers across the country would begin to understand, finally, that it was change-or-die time when it comes to creating a workplace that actually works for its women employees. That's how!

"Okay," she said, still sounding dubious (and me getting more irked by the second). "But none of this is going to change the fact that people still see motherhood as a 'lesser-than' job. I mean, it's not like it will make my husband suddenly see doing the laundry as equally important or start paying attention to when our kids need new sneakers."

Ouch. She was absolutely correct. At that point I did quickly finish my drink and slunk off, the wind taken out of my sails.

I've been working as an activist for most of my adult life, so policies and institutions were where I always believed change needed to be generated. But the more I thought about it, the more I realized that while the government and the workforce absolutely have to implement changes, *so do the rest of us*. We all have to do our part so that these systemic changes we are fighting for happen across all sectors. I started to envision this as a house: The governmental support would lay the foundation that made the structure possible, employers could erect a stable frame and build walls, floors, and ceilings that give the house a workable structure, but it would take the inhabitants to bring the place to life. Without us, it's just an empty shell. If you've ever walked past a completed new construction before anyone moves in, you know the hollowness I'm talking about.

Mainstream feminism made the mistake the first time around of failing to address the domestic work mothers do and forgetting about fighting for equality in *all* the roles women play. We can't make the same mistake this time. The house won't survive the winds of change if we don't bolster it from the inside. Whether you identify as a woman, man, or nonbinary, this fight belongs to *all* of us. The changes need to happen in our minds and homes as much as they do out there in the world, to construct a house that is not only structurally sound, but livable in the long term.

CHANGING PERCEPTIONS ABOUT WOMEN, WORK, AND MOTHERHOOD

I don't know a secret magic formula for how we upend a century's worth of perception of women and motherhood. But as someone who has made it her life's work to disrupt the status quo, what I do know is this: Any and all change starts with awareness. We can't change anything ingrained—be it a systemic problem, a thought, habit, or belief—until we first root it out and take a good, hard, clear-eyed look at it in the light of day.

Concurrent with the pandemic, 2020, as we all know, saw

a long overdue cultural awakening to the systemic racism in our country. Millions of Americans were forced to hold up a mirror to examine their own deeply rooted biases and took action to educate themselves on what they did not truly know or understand about what it felt like to be a person of color in this country. To be clear: I am in no way comparing the discrimination against mothers in America to the daily injustices faced by people of color. What I am pointing to here is the methodology of each individual examining their biases as a way to begin to right a systemic wrong.

Shifting the perception of working women with children needs to start by checking our hidden mom biases. We already know from studies, statistics, and anecdotal evidence that employers view mothers as less competent and less committed to their jobs, and that the mothering work in all its demanding messiness is deemed as unappealing, boring, or not terribly worthy of adult respect. It's easy to shrug that off as nonsense that's offensive to both employers and women, but research backs up the argument that we've got some serious bias rooting out to do.

A massive worldwide study done in 2018, for instance, showed that one of the oldest (and most infuriating) myths about motherhood is alive and kicking: that children and family lives will suffer if women work. Another report published by a team of researchers from multiple universities showed that men who have stay-at-home wives (ostensibly to raise the children) are more likely than those with working wives to harbor negative beliefs about women in the workforce. They view workplaces with women leaders as less appealing and consider female candidates to be less qualified for promotion than their male counterparts. The report also showed that men who stand in the way of advancing women in their own workplaces are "more likely to populate the upper echelons of organizations and thus, occupy more powerful positions." A belief that starts at the top is almost guaranteed to permeate the entire culture of an organization.

Okay, so that's the research. But what do *you* think? Yes, I'm talking directly to you. What are your opinions about mothers' roles, capacities, and value?

I wasn't surprised that I had a hard time getting men to talk about this issue. In our hyper politically correct climate, they're understandably loath to fess up to anything that carries even a whiff of misogyny—and rightly so. Plus, I don't know about the men you know, but the last thing pretty much any guy I know wants to do is insult his mom! What I did hear from several men who were willing to open up a bit on this issue was that the ideology of mother = sacrifice was pretty baked into their psyches. A tech entrepreneur in his late thirties summarized it pretty much on the nose: "My mother did everything for me—still does. I think that's kind of just how moms are."

The roots of that belief run *deep*—as in fundamentally, psychically deep. In its breakdown of the four female archetypes (maiden, mother, wild-woman, wise woman) explored and propagated in everything from popular films to fairy tales, the well-known screenwriting source creativescreen writing.com defines the mother as "the keeper of the hearth, the businesswoman who works all day and takes care of the house at night, and the worker in the field with a papoose across her chest. Her responsibilities are so vast and evolving, it is a shame, but also no surprise, that we often take her for granted or expect sacrifice even after she has already sacrificed." Given the vast impact of popular culture in shaping our views, it's no wonder mothers are expected to be bottomless, multitasking givers who require no support in return.

What did surprise me was that the individuals who came out with the most shocking admissions of judgment about mothers were women themselves.

Kelly is a media executive at an international publishing company. She's always super put-together and has whatever the newest, sexiest tech gadget is. When her first daughter started school, Kelly would get dressed for work and then do drop-off every morning—a parenting scene that is rife with hierarchy in New York City. "I'm embarrassed to admit this," she said with a grimace, "but I used to look at the full-time moms with pity. I would judge them for walking around in workout pants all day and sitting outside the bagel place in a gaggle for an hour after drop-off. I remember one time I was watching one of the stay-at-home moms reading an email on her phone looking exasperated and I actually consciously formulated the thought, 'Oh, what happened . . . did your Mommy and Me class get canceled today?' So bitchy."

I asked Kelly what changed and without missing a beat she said, "COVID. I swear that year at home trying to work while my kids were there made me realize these women were working just as hard if not harder than I do all day."

Maria, a mother of three from Los Angeles who works part-time as a legal secretary, referred to herself as a "self-hating mom." She told me she took great pains to not do "mom-ish" things like going to PTA meetings or finding crushed up Goldfish crackers in her coat pockets. The avoidance of association with being "mom-ish" spoke volumes.

Women don't come to these disparaging viewpoints on their own; far from it. The judgments aimed at women surrounding their responsibilities as a mother are pervasive. Monica Hesse, a columnist for the *Washington Post*, wrote a piece detailing the compelling reasons why she chose for a long time not to have children, not the least of which were the impossible expectations of sacrifice. She hit the nail on the head in describing the ingrained notion that motherhood is a choice and therefore we should just stop boring everyone with our "whining" about how pregnancy and childbirth are painful, messy endeavors that require stamina and patience to heal from, or about the gross lack of caregiving support. "I did not have children because America is a difficult place to be a mom," she wrote. "And because every policy-based attempt to change that is met by telling women to buck up, drink a glass of rosé and download the Calm app. Screw that."

Then, of course, there are the unexamined (and insanely

misguided) notions that many of us hold about our own superhuman capacities. I am embarrassed to admit that I myself perpetuated the myth that "having it all" was possible for a long time. Back when I was preaching loud and proud the Gospel of Professional Ambition, I would urge women in speech after speech to step through their fears and unleash their full career potential. A shiny brass ring was right in front of them; all they had to do was grab it. While I always acknowledged to some extent the historical inequities, my gospel was that even though these structural inequities exist, we have to give women strategies to thrive in the culture as it is. My speeches put the onus on women not to examine the systemic problems but to fix themselves.

After these rousing speeches, I'd often be approached by bright-eyed young women who would tell me they were on board, they wanted it all! Some of them would try to pin me down and ask me, a bit tentatively, how to balance work and family life. I think about this now with a bit of shame. Because at the time, I waved away their concerns.

Actually waved.

With my hand.

Worse, at the time, those questions actually irritated me. To me, these female concerns seemed . . . minimal. Not the real problem or impediment. I'd say breezily, "Just go for it and family life will sort itself out."

I can't justify this except to say that that is what I actually thought. I'd bought into the Big Lie. From the swish of my glossy blowout to the tips of my stylish slingbacks, I believed that. At least back then. Within a few years, when that glossy blowout was replaced with a messy mom bun (that may or may not have had dried bits of pureed sweet potatoes in it) and the slingbacks were traded in for sneakers so I could speed-walk from my apartment to my office and back every day, I realized the injustice I'd done these women by airbrushing over the competing demands of working motherhood.

It's on all of us—whether we identify as men, women, or neither—to get real about the beliefs we hold and the stories we tell about women, work, and motherhood. First, so we can shift our own thinking, and then, even more crucially, so we can encourage others to do the same.

9

ADVOCATE: From Rage
to Power

*Our policymaking has not accounted for the fact
that people's work lives and their personal lives are
inextricably linked, and if one suffers so does
the other.*

—TREASURY SECRETARY JANET YELLEN

When I wrote the original op-ed outlining a Marshall Plan for Moms, it was November 2020 and we were in the darkest throes of the pandemic. Women were sinking hard and fast as childcare responsibilities squeezed us out of the workforce and lay waste to our careers, our bank accounts, and our mental health. At the heart of that rescue plan was a callout to the government for a critical monthly payment for mothers of $2,400 per month, to keep them afloat through the pandemic. We told then president-elect Biden that while other countries have social safety nets, America instead has moms, and it's time to compensate mothers for all they do to keep our economy and our country running. That it was time to *pay up*. And yes, it was controversial.

With the worst of the pandemic hopefully in the rearview mirror, we now must turn our sights to what is needed in the long term to rebuild the workforce in a way that makes work and motherhood sustainable for all women. As Dr. C. Nicole Mason, president and chief executive officer of the Institute for Women's Policy Research, wrote, "One of the most important ways we can make a difference is pushing for legislation that helps women get back to work and keep from falling further behind. Now is the time to think boldly about what it will take to build a more equitable society—one where women have opportunities to reach their full potential without harm or barriers."

This chapter outlines the three critical public policies that we as women need lawmakers to put in place with a sense of urgency: affordable childcare, guaranteed and paid parental leave, and continued cash payments to mothers (and parents). While this list is not exhaustive, and there are other structural changes needed to economically support women, including changes to our tax code, Social Security, pay equity, pre-K, public health, and ending harassment and discrimination in the workplace, for the purposes of this book I want to focus on those three.

Still, as critical as these policies are, they will not solve the deeply rooted norms that make women our default caregivers in the first place. The battle against those norms—against our hugely damaging structural inequities—doesn't end with just structural support from the government. As discussed in the previous chapters, there is a wholesale reweaving of the social fabric we must all undertake. What might end as a result of these public policies, though, or at least begin to abate, is the gross disregard for the value of mothers' unpaid, unseen, unappreciated labor. It will send a hugely important signal to girls and young women across the country who are the next generation of our workforce and parents that our society values the contributions of women and that their careers, dreams, and lives will not be taken for granted.

I hope that reading this will give every woman the facts, voice, and courage she needs to join this important fight.

AFFORDABLE CHILDCARE

My parents came to this country as refugees. As they were building their life, like many parents, they found childcare to be too expensive given their limited means. When I was in elementary school and my sister was beginning middle school, my parents could no longer afford the fifty dollars a week to pay for a sitter. So, my sister and I became latchkey kids. Every day after school we would walk the ten blocks home, let ourselves in, make ourselves grilled cheese in the toaster oven, and be entertained by the new babysitter: the television. We learned about being an American family from Carol, Mike, and their six kids on *The Brady Bunch* and the Huxtables on *The Cosby Show*. Yet weirdly, none of those kids ever seemed to be by themselves every afternoon.

My parents' story is not an anomaly. Childcare is too expensive for most families. The average family with at least one child today under age five needs to spend thirteen percent of their family income on childcare; the U.S. Department of Health and Human Services defines affordable childcare as costing no more than seven percent. For some parents, their childcare costs are almost double what they pay monthly for their mortgage. For others, a mortgage is a luxury they can only dream of having, and some are forced to take desperate measures. The hearts of millions of people around the country broke for the single mother in Ohio who was forced to leave her two children, ages nine and three, alone in a motel room because she had to go to her job in a nearby pizza shop to earn enough to feed the family and could not afford any semblance of childcare. She was arrested on child endangerment charges and later released; a GoFundMe page set up by her community raised more than $100,000 to help her buy a home.

Not everyone gets rescued. People of color, unsurprisingly, are hit the hardest by childcare costs since many Black and Latina women are already in low-paying jobs. A 2016 survey reported that cost was the primary impediment for Black women and Latinas seeking quality childcare. The current benefits provided don't solve the cost issue. Only fourteen percent of children who are eligible to receive publicly funded childcare subsidies actually receive them; in most cases the amount is too low in any event to support the cost of quality childcare.

For many families in this country, regardless of race or ethnicity, childcare is hard to find. More than half of Americans live in "childcare deserts," in which there are licensed care slots for only one out of every three children. Low-income and rural families are most likely to live in these underserved areas. Studies show that Black mothers are more likely to live in these childcare deserts and suffer the double whammy of having jobs with less flexibility.

Childcare is hard to find because there is a shortage of quality childcare providers. For as crucial as we in this country say our children are, childcare workers are among the most underpaid workers in America. To put this in perspective, they earn less than people who care for animals in zoos or homes. A 2021 report from the Center for the Study of Child Care Employment at the University of California, Berkeley, showed that workers in only ten out of fifty states earn enough to cover their basic needs without having to turn to public assistance or a second job. The median yearly pay for early-childhood workers of $25,460 brings them below the current federal poverty level of $26,200 for a family of four. The majority of childcare workers are women, many of whom are women of color, bringing racial inequity into the equation.

The dismal wages of these professions have made them unappealing to American workers, causing a reverberating effect for the rest of the labor force. As a May 2021 article from the Center for American Progress neatly summarized, "Childcare is the work that enables all other work."

Finally, the lack of affordable and available childcare is a strain on the economy. Employers lose approximately $375 to $500 per working-age adult per year because of absences and turnover due to breakdowns in childcare. In response, echoing what so many working parents feel on a daily basis, Treasury Secretary Janet Yellen lamented, "The free market works well in many different sectors, but childcare is not one of them." It's time for that to change. The upshot of the U.S. Department of the Treasury September 2021 report: "Increasing access to high-quality, affordable childcare is essential to investing in the future of the American labor force."

Access to affordable, quality childcare is good for parents, it's good for children, and it's good for the economy. Parents need reliable childcare in order to work. Period. Most notably working mothers need it, as they are the primary workers who are forced to leave their paid work for unpaid caregiving when childcare is not affordable. Children need quality childcare to nurture their early brain development, much of which happens before the age of five. And society needs quality, affordable childcare to sustain our economy. Researchers estimate that every $1 invested in quality early-childhood education yields nine times that in positive results for society. Children who attend early-childhood education or care programs continue on in school longer, commit fewer crimes, which saves judicial system dollars, and are less prone to illness over their lifetimes, which in turn puts less burden on the healthcare industry. According to an S&P report, the United States could increase its gross domestic product (GDP) by $1.6 trillion if women in America entered and remained in the workplace at a rate equal to that of women in Norway, where the government subsidizes childcare.

The United States trails other nations in terms of providing affordable childcare. Other wealthy countries contribute as much as $29,726 per year toward childcare of children age two and under. The United States contributes $500. Toddlers in Denmark are guaranteed a spot in care centers; Danish parents need to pay only one-quarter of the tuition cost. If the parents opt to hire an in-home caregiver, the government will pay for that as well. The United States has no subsidies for care-center or in-home childcare. In France, parents receive tax credits as high as eighty-five percent of the cost of hiring in-home care or attending a childcare center.

This dichotomy is not only bewildering, it undermines the financial stability of millions of families, stymying economic recovery by preventing women from reentering the workforce, and threatening our ability to compete on the global stage.

The United States came close once before to passing a bill that would have made childcare affordable. In 1971, a supermajority of senators voted for a national day-care system. There was large-scale bipartisan support for the bill. The

House of Representatives then passed the measure, albeit by a smaller margin. But then President Richard Nixon suddenly announced he was visiting China. After his announcement, opponents began casting the bill for childcare in the harsh light of the Cold War as "the Sovietization of American children." Since President Nixon was running for reelection and his trip to China was getting a lot of blowback, he vetoed the bill and it landed in the dustbin, recast in the unfavorable light of government meddling with the minds of our youngest and most vulnerable.

That was a big swing and a miss that we cannot afford to repeat.

The childcare bill introduced by the Biden administration ensures that no family ever has to pay more than seven percent of their income for childcare. It provides support for struggling childcare centers who were forced to close during the pandemic, exacerbating the already brewing childcare crisis. It provides funding for early-childhood education and care workers, including guaranteed wage increases and money for professional development and scholarships to obtain education credentials. Finally, it provides universal, free pre-K for all children. We as a country would never stop funding public education, yet there is overwhelming evidence that the first four years of a child's life are the most important in terms of cognitive and emotional development.

PAID PARENTAL LEAVE

There is family leave in the United States. You can take up to twelve weeks to spend time with your newborn. You won't be paid. Oh, you also have to have worked at the same job for at least a year, worked for at least 1,250 hours in that year, and your employer has to have fifty employees, all who work within seventy-five miles of one another. And presto. Family leave. Hope you have some savings, and more than what you had to pay for the actual birth of your child. (Average cost of having a baby: approximately $10,000.)

In other words: There is no family leave in the United States.

And moms have paid the price for not having paid family leave. Tara, a mother of one from Washington, felt extreme pressure to return to her job in an automotive salesroom after delivering her son, Cody. Within two weeks of her returning home from the hospital, her boss started calling with questions and requests for her to handle paperwork. His impatience when she said she would get to it after the baby went to sleep came through loud and clear in nonverbal cues like heavy sighs. "I felt like I needed to get back there to preserve my job," Tara said. "My family needs that income. So I went back just four weeks after Cody was born. For a long, long time I felt horrible about missing out on those early days with him. I had to give up breastfeeding because there was nowhere private at work that I could pump, and I worried that I cheated him out of all those health benefits of breastfeeding. I don't know if the sadness I felt was true postpartum depression because I didn't have the time to find a therapist, but I'm pretty sure it wasn't far off."

Many, many other countries have paid family leave. The Czech Republic offers twenty-eight paid weeks. Italy offers five months. Canada has seventeen weeks. These are not necessarily reserved just for the mother. One hundred twenty countries offer some kind of family leave paid for by the government.

Paid leave, like affordable childcare, has a wide range of positive effects for families, workers, employers, and the economy. As we touched on in the previous chapter, children whose parents are home to care for them in the first few months of their lives experience myriad health benefits, ranging from greater rates of immunization to lower rates of infant mortality. Mothers who take twelve weeks or more of paid parental leave experience lower rates of postpartum depression, as evidenced in reverse by Tara's story. On the whole, parents who take paid, job-guaranteed family leave are happier and remain more committed to their employers, which in turn creates less turnover. Remember the study out of Rutgers that showed that women who take paid leave are ninety-three percent more likely to still be in the workforce nine to twelve months later than women who don't? A great example of a company thinking along the right lines here is Google. Google found that postpartum women were exiting the company twice as often as other employees. They expanded their paid leave policy from three months of partially paid to five months of fully paid and saw the attrition rate go down by fifty percent.

Conversely, not having a national policy of paid leave comes at a steep cost. Lack of access to paid family and medical leave costs working families an estimated $22.5 billion in wages per year. And these costs affect us all. Women who are not given access to paid leave are forty percent more likely to require public assistance the first year after giving birth than women who go back to work after taking paid leave.

MONTHLY PAYMENTS TO MOMS

When I first introduced the Marshall Plan for Moms, we called on the Biden administration and Congress to pay moms $2,400 a month for their unseen, unpaid labor. It caused a ton of hoopla. But hear me out, because the idea of paying mothers for their invisible work is not a crazy idea.

Why $2,400? Good question. At the time, the government had set unemployment at $600 per week, and given how mothers had seen their paid labor at work supplanted by unpaid labor at home, that seemed like a good starting point. But the amount was never the point. The point was that if economists could crunch the numbers and put a dollar value on the cost of shutting down businesses, or schools, or replacing HVAC systems, they needed to put a dollar value on what moms were giving up, and what they were putting in. And pay us for it.

In 1965, women in America did almost ALL the unpaid

work at home. The cooking, cleaning, childcare, and running of the family enterprise. The gap between what men and women do on the home front has narrowed, but in 2020 women still spent thirty-seven percent more time doing unpaid domestic work—and, unlike 1965, they do it while maintaining their full-time jobs. We need policies that are going to help get that ratio to 50/50.

Why does valuing this unpaid work matter? First, if we ever want to achieve gender equality in the workplace, we have to achieve gender equality at home. Working men who have a female partner in the home have a competitive advantage over working women because their partner is taking care of the domestic work at home, freeing men up to focus on their paid work. And this is far from a recent development. In the eighteenth century, economist and moral philosopher Adam Smith lived at his mother's house while writing *The Wealth of Nations*. She cooked, cleaned, and did all his laundry. Interesting how the man who defined the basic principles for how we conceptualize a country's economy left out the contribution that made his work possible in the first place.

Domestic work has value. But until we as a society put a number on it, *we will never really value care work.*

Second, we must put cash in the hands of mothers if we ever want to make a dent in poverty. Women—particularly women of color—are more likely to live in poverty, are overrepresented in low-paying occupations, and are far more likely to lack access to sick leave and healthcare benefits. Black women are paid 62 cents for every dollar a white man is paid, and Latina women make even less at 54 cents. In addition to the urgent need to pass paid family leave and affordable child-care, we must also compensate mothers for their unpaid labor to even out the gross disparities.

Finally, as we look to rebuild from the Great Resignation and the recession triggered by the pandemic, our economy will be made far stronger when all workers who want to work at their fullest potential are able to. According to Oxfam, close to half of women across the globe are not able to participate in the formal economy because of their care responsibilities. As a global leader, we must take the strong stand that that number is simply unacceptable.

Here's the part that's even more controversial, but I believe even more crucial: These cash payments must be paid to all moms, whether they are currently participating in the labor force or not. Why? Because that will finally give mothers the choice and freedom to move in and out of the workforce without penalty.

Many countries already directly show the value they place on the unpaid labor of mothers. According to the University of Antwerp's Minimum Income Protection Indicators database, as of 2012 at least eleven wealthy countries instituted what they call "parental or child allowances": Austria, Denmark, Finland, France, Germany, Ireland, Luxembourg, the Netherlands, Norway, Sweden, and the UK. Some of these benefits are universal and some are means-tested (meaning your income determines your eligibility).

Unfortunately, the United States has a long history of resistance toward parent allowances that were not tied to work because some politicians felt that cash allowances disincentivize formal work. The Child Tax Credit (CTC) that was passed as a part of the American Rescue Plan Act of 2021 changed this American ideology. It was signed into law by President Biden in March 2021, just two months after he took office. I believe that the CTC is a critical and positive first step—a "down payment," if you will—on shifting ideology and compensating mothers for their unpaid labor.

The Child Tax Credit was actually first introduced in 1998. However, the way it worked was that the government determined how much money a family got based on how much it owed in taxes. That left out many poor people who were disproportionately Black and Hispanic who did not pay enough taxes to get a credit or who didn't pay taxes at all because they were not in the formal economy. The Biden administration rectified this by turning the CTC from a "tax deduction" to be used at the time of filing taxes into an ongoing cash transfer administered by the IRS irrespective of whether you paid taxes. Every family would receive $3,000 to $3,600 per child a year. This money was a lifesaver for many to purchase necessities and cover ongoing living expenses in the face of high unemployment and furloughs that occurred early on in the pandemic.

As of the time this book is being written, the Biden administration is working to make the CTC that was instituted during the pandemic as permanent as possible, which will give critical help to mothers. While the CTC is being sold as a program to help cut child poverty, we also know that the permanent expansion of the CTC will provide critical relief to mothers who are juggling needs at home—including serving as de facto teachers and nannies—with demands at work or while trying to get back into the workforce.

As mothers, we say loud and clear: We need help. This is a step in the right direction.

WHAT WOMEN CAN DO

Since the early days of the feminist movement, we've seen the powerful changes women can affect when they band together to demand change. And we've seen a glimpse of what can happen when mothers, specifically, harness the full strength of our numbers. Think of Moms Demand Action, which has changed the conversation and legislation around gun violence; of Mothers Against Drunk Driving, which has helped decrease driving deaths by fifty-five percent; of the millions of moms who decided the 2020 election in support of those who support us. Now it's time we advocate for ourselves.

This is where the feminist movement left off, as it forgot that in its formidable push for equality in the workplace that we also needed to push for equality in the home via compensation for the unpaid labor we do. That all mothers matter, whether they are in the formal or informal economy. Whether they are moms who stay at home, work part-time, or occupy the corner office. All women—whether we are mothers or not—must throw their weight behind getting these important public policies passed.

Look, I know we're tired, so I am not telling you to add one more thing to your plate and get out there to march or strike. Not just yet, but possibly soon, we can take a page from our sisters who organized the historic Icelandic March in 1975 that transformed the economic lives of millions of women. On October 24, 1975, the women of Iceland went on strike to demonstrate the indispensable work of women for Iceland's economy and society. They called it the "Women's Day Off," and almost ninety percent of women in the country participated. They did not go to work. They did not do the laundry, or take care of the children, or cook dinner. Factories closed. Fathers were forced to bring their kids to work. The country ground to a halt. Quite literally, it did not function. As a result, within a year, the legislature passed equal pay. Changes with real and lasting impact happened because these brave women gave their partners, employers, and children a taste of what the world would be like if we didn't work. Someday soon, in whatever organized way we can, we need to do the same.

And while we're all tired, we're also all pissed off, so let's channel that into a force for change in any way we can. Use your voice in small ways and big ways. Vote. Write to your senators and congresspeople. Get involved and educated on public policies that make your life better. Engage your communities.

Educate the people in your life on what you learned here. Sign up on www.marshallplanformoms.com so you're with us and ready when we take big action to show the world how vitally important the work we do as women really is.

This is how we as women take ourselves out of rage and into power.

Afterword

The subtitle of this book states that the future of women and work is different than we might think. But how so?

Because it's not about breaking more glass ceilings. It's not about achieving gender parity, or even equal pay. It's about a full-scale reenvisioning of how we as a society, a workforce, and a country define "work" and the value we place on the invisible labor women do outside the workplace that holds our economy and our social fabric together. It's a systemic revision that calls on not just women but everyone who depends on us—our families, our employers, and our government—to step out of the grossly outdated models and into the workplace of the future.

The phrase "workplace of the future" may sound like a fantasy, but with the upheaval triggered by COVID-19, we fast-forwarded into that far-off unknown void at lightning speed. As with all the important inflection points this country has hit, we find ourselves at a critical crossroads: Do we continue on as we always have or do we confront the reality that the future of work requires a different approach?

We can sit back and allow the advancements of half a century of feminism to be eradicated along with the viability of our entire economy. We can sit back and watch working women be pushed out of the labor force and have their dreams die on the vine. We can sit back and watch our labor force continue to shrink, continuing the death spiral of job vacancies set in motion by the pandemic. We can be complacent in the face of a mental health crisis affecting millions of working women that will undoubtedly grow from alarming to catastrophic if not reversed, and we can give up on the innovation capital of one-half of our country's population.

Or, we can band together to make the deep systemic changes needed in our workplaces, our society, our cultural narrative, and our public policies to support the valuable contributions of women at home and to the paid labor force. We can pay up and give mothers the flexibility, compensation, support, and respect that they deserve so they no longer need to hide the critical care work they do at home. We can create a society in which paid parental leave and access to affordable, high-quality childcare are viewed and supported as the backbone of the American family and reweave the social fabric to change "equality" to mean equality in all sectors, not just the workplace. We can prioritize women's mental health and se-cure the well-being—dare I even say existence—of the next generation.

We can finish this once and for all. I've given you the plan. What's it going to be?

Acknowledgments

This book was a journey that I feel blessed to have taken. What started with a global pandemic that upended my life and those of millions of other women ultimately ended with a life-changing realization: that this crisis has afforded us a once-in-a-generation opportunity to change the entire landscape of working motherhood in this country.

This book would *NOT* have happened without my writing partner, Debra Goldstein. As a mother who has gone through so many of the challenges I write about, she was the only person with whom I could imagine making this meaningful exploration of working motherhood. Her brilliance, her commitment to excellence, and her ability to take complicated topics and render them accessible make her truly a one of a kind writer. As an activist and a movement builder, it was an honor to write this book with her because I know that due to our collaboration, this work will make the impact we are aiming for. Debra, you are the only person I want to be with in the writing trenches.

Thank you, Richard Pine, the best literary agent in the world. You encouraged me to go deeper and to write a big-idea book about working motherhood. You exemplify what it means to be a male ally to women in struggle. Thank you for your epic kindness. Thanks to William Callahan for being a thought partner and for your unparalleled research skills. And, of course, thank you to Eliza Rothstein and the amazing team at Inkwell. I am happy to call you family!

Thank you to Jonathan Karp, Libby McGuire, and the incredible team at Simon & Schuster. Thank you to my editor, Julia Cheiffetz, and her team: Amara Balan, Nicholas Ciani, and Joanna Pinsker. Julia and I met in 2010 when I was just an upstart insurgent running for Congress. She saw something in me that I didn't see in myself. Almost twelve years later, she encouraged me to write this book for all the moms who needed an advocate, pushing us to go deeper even when we thought we were done. Her sage advice made this book a critical read for employers and working moms.

Thank you to Gloria Noel for being my right hand in putting this book together. Your research, analysis, and encouragement got me to the finish line. And thank you to Charlotte Stone for your critical mind and marketing brilliance in getting this book into the hands of every person who needs to read it.

This book was inspired by the Marshall Plan for Moms. Thank you to Deborah Singer, Charlotte Stone, and Gloria Noel for helping build the Marshall Plan for Moms movement. What started as a few women making good trouble has led to an international conversation about how we value women's paid and unpaid labor. And thank you to Mara Bolis for taking a leap and joining our small, mighty team to lead this movement into the future.

Thank you to Whitney Peeling of Broadside PR who believed in this book and me. I'm so grateful for your vision and support.

Thank you to Peg Tyre for your tireless work on this book and for being my sister-in-arms in thinking big about what an equitable workplace could look like.

Thank you to the incredible team at APCO Impact for your partnership in the Marshall Plan for Moms playbook, *Making Workplaces Work for Moms*, that informed many of this book's recommendations. Thank you to Elizabeth Duncan-Watt, Akinyi Ochieng, and Denielle Sachs for your leadership and advocacy.

Thanks to all the moms who have joined our movement to go from rage to power. To all the women who feel unseen, I see you and will always fight for you.

Thank you to my mother, Meena, and my sister, Keshma, who taught me how to be a mother. To Maya and Surina, this book is for you, so you don't have to struggle the way so many before you have. Thank you to Audrey Johnson Clarke who has cared for my sons, Shaan and Sai. Nothing I have achieved is possible without your support and work.

To the male allies in my life—my husband, Nihal; my sons, Shaan and Sai; and my dad—thank you for being my biggest champions. Nihal, thank you for allowing me to practice my strategies on you and for engaging in fights that have put these questions into perspective. For Shaan and Sai, I hope your world is more equitable and that you blossom into the advocating, kind, generous male allies I already see you becoming.

Notes

Introduction: We (I) Screwed Up

12 *my unwashed dishes:* Aneesa Bodiat, "No, I'm Not 'Just' a Stay-at-Home Mom," *The New York Times*, April 17, 2020, https://www.nytimes.com/2020/04/17/parenting/stay-at-home-mom.html.

14 *considerably and inequitably:* Laura M. Giurge, Ashley V. Whillans, and Ayse Yemiscigil, "A Multicountry Perspective on Gender Differences in Time Use During COVID-19," Proceedings of the National Academy of Sciences of the United States of America, 118 (12), 2021, https://doi.org/10.1073/pnas.2018494118.

14 *twelve* additional days *of chores:* Ashley Whillans on Twitter, https://twitter.com/ashleywhillans/status/1369076103319597062?s=20.

14 *happiness and mental health:* William K. Goodman, Ashley M. Geiger, and Jutta M. Wolf, "Leisure Activities Are Linked to Mental Health Benefits by Providing Time Structure: Comparing Employed, Unemployed and Homemakers," *Journal of Epidemiology and Community Health* 71 (1), 2017, https://doi.org/10.1136/jech-2016-207260.

14 *twenty-five percent jump:* Maxime Taquet, Emily A. Holmes, and
    Paul J. Harrison, "Depression and Anxiety Disorders During the
    COVID-19 Pandemic: Knowns and Unknowns," *The Lancet* 398
    (10312), 2021, https://doi.org/10.1016/S0140-6736(21)02221-2.

14 *women's alcohol consumption:* Michael S. Pollard, Joan S. Tucker,
    and Harold D. Green Jr., "Changes in Adult Alcohol Use and
    Consequences During the COVID-19 Pandemic in the US," *JAMA
    Network Open,* 2020, doi:10.1001/jamanetworkopen.2020.22942.

15 *four times the number of men:* "Parents at the Best Workplaces:
    The Largest-Ever Study of Working Parents," Maven, 2020, https:
    //info.mavenclinic.com/pdf/parents-at-the-best-workplaces
    ?submissionGuid=5ac95855-8079-46ac-9ba5-f8b11c2ae5c5.

15 *"The Great Resignation":* Juliana Kaplan, "The Psychologist
    Who Coined the Phrase 'Great Resignation' Reveals How He
    Saw It Coming and Where He Sees It Going," *Business Insider,*
    October 2, 2021, https://www.businessinsider.com/why-every
    one-is-quitting-great-resignation-psychologist-pandemic
    -rethink-life-2021-10.

15 *more so women of color:* Ember Smith and Richard V. Reeves, "Black
    Moms Facing the Toughest Childcare Crunch: How Policy Can
    Help," Brookings, February 24, 2021, https://www.brookings.edu
    /blog/how-we-rise/2021/02/24/black-moms-facing-the-toughest
    -childcare-crunch-how-policy-can-help/.

15 *"not because their jobs have vanished":* Abby Vesoulis, "'If We Had a
    Panic Button, We'd Be Hitting It.' Women Are Exiting the Labor
    Force En Masse—and That's Bad for Everyone," *Time,* October 17,
    2020, https://time.com/5900583/women-workforce-economy
    -covid/.

16 *twice that of men of the same age:* Jonnelle Marte, "Women Left
    U.S. Workforce Last Month, but in Fewer Numbers Than a
    Year Ago," Reuters, October 8, 2021, https://www.reuters.com
    /business/women-left-us-workforce-last-month-fewer-numbers
    -than-year-ago-2021-10-08/.

16 *women held more payroll jobs than men:* "The Employment

Situation—October 2021," Bureau of Labor Statistics, November 2021, https://www.bls.gov/news.release/pdf/empsit.pdf.

17 *Today that number is at seventy percent:* Joan C. Williams and Heather Boushey, "The Three Faces of Work-Family Conflict," The Center for American Progress, January 25, 2010, https://www.americanprogress.org/article/the-three-faces-of-work-family-conflict/.

17 *a serious labor shortage:* Paul Krugman, "The Revolt of the American Worker," *The New York Times,* October 14, 2021, https://www.nytimes.com/2021/10/14/opinion/workers-quitting-wages.html.

18 *hide half of ourselves:* Jessica Grose, " 'I Cry on Tuesdays and Fridays'," *The New York Times*, March 25, 2021, https://www.nytimes.com/2021/03/24/parenting/moms-coronavirus-mental-health.html.

Chapter 1: Something Has to Give

23 *lay waste to our ambition:* Courtney Connley, "Women's Ambition Plummeted During the Coronavirus Pandemic, as Careers Stalled and Burnout Spiked," CNBC, March 9, 2021, https://www.cnbc.com/2021/03/09/65percent-of-working-women-say-pandemic-has-made-things-worse-at-work.html.

23 *our relationships:* W. Bradford Wilcox, Lyman Stone, and Wendy Wang, "The Good and Bad News About Marriage in the Time of COVID," The Institute for Family Studies, September 22, 2020, https://ifstudies.org/blog/the-good-and-bad-news-about-marriage-in-the-time-of-covid.

23 *any other industrialized nation:* International Labour Organization, "Americans Work Longest Hours Among Industrialized Countries . . . ," ILO.org, September 6, 1999, https://www.ilo.org/global/about-the-ilo/newsroom/news/WCMS_071326/lang--en/index.htm.

23 *we pay the price:* Centers for Disease Control and Prevention, "About Mental Health," https://www.cdc.gov/mentalhealth/learn/index.htm.

23 *more than forty hours:* CreditLoan, "The State of the 40-Hour
Workweek," CreditLoan blog, January 14, 2019, https://www
.creditloan.com/blog/the-state-of-the-40-hour-workweek/.

24 *two hours more per day:* Institute for Women's Policy Research,
"Women Do 2 More Hours of Housework Daily Than Men,"
January 22, 2020, https://iwpr.org/media/press-hits/women
-do-2-more-hours-of-housework-daily-than-men/.

24 *heavy caretaking and financial needs:* Kim Parker and Eileen Pat-
ten, "The Sandwich Generation," Pew Research Center,
January 30, 2013, https://www.pewresearch.org/social-trends
/2013/01/30/the-sandwich-generation/.

24 *don't have time to think about dating:* Lisa Bonos and Emily Guskin,
"It's Not Just You: New Data Shows More Than Half of Young
People in America Don't Have a Romantic Partner," *The Washington Post,* March 21, 2019, https://www.washingtonpost.com
/lifestyle/2019/03/21/its-not-just-you-new-data-shows-more
-than-half-young-people-america-dont-have-romantic-partner/.

25 *more than half of Black mothers:* A. W. Geiger, Gretchen Livingston,
and Kristen Bialik, "6 Facts About U.S. Moms," Pew Research
Center, May 8, 2019, https://www.pewresearch.org/fact-tank
/2019/05/08/facts-about-u-s-mothers/.

25 *"childcare deserts":* Ember Smith and Richard V. Reeves, "Black
Moms Facing the Toughest Childcare Crunch: How Policy Can
Help," Brookings, February 24, 2021, https://www.brookings
.edu/blog/how-we-rise/2021/02/24/black-moms-facing-the
-toughest-childcare-crunch-how-policy-can-help/.

25 *women are the primary breadwinners:* A. W. Geiger, Gretchen
Livingston, and Kristen Bialik, "6 Facts About U.S. Moms,"
Pew Research Center, May 8, 2019, https://www.pewresearch
.org/fact-tank/2019/05/08/facts-about-u-s-mothers/.

27 *suffering from extreme burnout:* "Parents at the Best Workplaces:
The Largest-Ever Study of Working Parents," Maven, 2020, https:
//info.mavenclinic.com/pdf/parents-at-the-best-workplaces
?submissionGuid=5ac95855-8079-46ac-9ba5-f8b11c2ae5c5.

28 *loss of our ambition:* Andrea Hsu, " 'This Is Too Much': Working Moms Are Reaching the Breaking Point During the Pandemic," NPR, September 29, 2020, https://www.npr.org/2020/09/29 /918127776/this-is-too-much-working-moms-are-reaching-the -breaking-point-during-the-pandemic.

36 *largest drop in marital happiness:* Belinda Luscombe, "Many Parents Are Happier Than Non-Parents—But Not in the U.S.," *Time,* https://time.com/collection/guide-to-happness/4370344/parents -happiness-children-study/.

37 *burned-out women and struggling moms:* Jessica Grose, Jessica Bennett, Melonyce McAfee, and Farah Miller, "America's Mothers Are in Crisis," *The New York Times,* February 4, 2021, https: //www.nytimes.com/interactive/2021/02/04/parenting/working -moms-coronavirus.html.

37 *lack of motivation:* Megan Leonhardt, "9.8 Million Working Mothers in the U.S. Are Suffering from Burnout," CNBC, December 3, 2020, https://www.cnbc.com/2020/12/03/millions -of-working-mothers-in-the-us-are-suffering-from-burnout.html.

37 *marked decrease in their mental health:* Linley Sanders, "Covid-19 Pandemic Has Had a Particularly Negative Impact on Mothers' Mental Health," YouGov, March 4, 2021, https://today.yougov .com/topics/education/articles-reports/2021/03/04/coronavirus -impact-on-mothers-mental-health.

38 *needed to stop mentioning their children:* Helen Lewis, "The Pandemic Has Given Women a New Kind of Rage," *The Atlantic,* March 2021, https://www.theatlantic.com/international/archive /2021/03/pandemic-has-made-women-angry/618239/.

38 *increased their drinking:* Aaron M. White, "Gender Differences in the Epidemiology of Alcohol Use and Related Harms in the United States," *Alcohol Research* 40 (2), October 2020, https: //arcr.niaaa.nih.gov/women-and-alcohol/gender-differences -epidemiology-alcohol-use-and-related-harms-united-states.

38 *"Mommy Juice":* Ibid.

39 *Close to twenty percent:* Alisha Haridasani Gupta, "Funding for

Start-Ups Founded by Women Is Surging," *The New York Times*, November 2, 2021, https://www.nytimes.com/2021/11/02 /business/dealbook/female-founded-startups-vc-funding.html.

40 *up fifty percent:* Carrie Blazina and Drew Desilver, "A Record Number of Women Are Serving in the 117th Congress," Pew Research Center, January 15, 2021, https://www.pewresearch .org/fact-tank/2021/01/15/a-record-number-of-women-are -serving-in-the-117th-congress/.

40 *One in four mothers go back to work:* Sarah Kliff, "1 in 4 American Moms Return to Work Within 2 Weeks of Giving Birth—Here's What It's Like," *Vox*, August 22, 2015, https://www.vox.com/2015 /8/21/9188343/maternity-leave-united-states.

40 *forty percent of our income:* Leila Schochet, "The Child Care Crisis Is Keeping Women Out of the Workforce," The Center for American Progress, March 28, 2019, https://www.americanprogress .org/article/child-care-crisis-keeping-women-workforce/.

42 *economic crisis rendered by the pandemic:* Aimee Picchi, "Americans Are Quitting Their Jobs—and Women Are Leading 'The Great Resignation'," CBS News, October 13, 2021, https://www .cbsnews.com/news/women-job-market-economy-jolts/.

Chapter 2: The Marshall Plan for Moms

47 *Paid Leave:* Jill Filipovic, "Free Female Labor Is the Plan," Jill .substack.com, October 27, 2021, https://jill.substack.com/p /free-female-labor-is-the-plan.

53 *so she can pay her bills:* Jodi Kantor, Karen Weise, and Grace Ashford, "Inside Amazon's Worst Human Resources Problem," *The New York Times*, October 24, 2021, https://www.nytimes.com /2021/10/24/technology/amazon-employee-leave-errors.html.

54 *anxiety, and depression skyrocketed:* Maddie Van Ness, "Covid-19 and Women's Mental Health: The Impact on Wellbeing, Disparities, and Future Implications," *Community Connection Magazine*, April 1, 2021, https://www.baylor.edu/communityconnection /news.php?action=story&story=222809.

54 *children with special needs:* Jessica Grose, "America's Mothers Are in Crisis," *The New York Times*, February 4, 2021, https://www.nytimes.com/2021/02/04/parenting/working-moms-mental-health-coronavirus.html.

54 *more likely to pause her day:* Rani Molla, "For Women, Remote Work Is a Blessing and a Curse," *Recode*, July 13, 2021, https://www.vox.com/recode/22568635/women-remote-work-home.

54 *thirty-seven percent of women:* Jonathan Emmett, Gunnar Schrah, Matt Schrimper, and Alexandra Wood, "COVID-19 and the Employee Experience: How Leaders Can Seize the Moment," McKinsey & Company, June 29, 2020, https://www.mckinsey.com/business-functions/people-and-organizational-performance/our-insights/covid-19-and-the-employee-experience-how-leaders-can-seize-the-moment.

55 *"We have never seen numbers":* Abby Vesoulis, "'If We Had a Panic Button, We'd Be Hitting It.' Women Are Exiting the Labor Force En Masse—and That's Bad for Everyone," *Time*, October 17, 2020, https://time.com/5900583/women-workforce-economy-covid/.

55 *The industries that employ mostly women:* Leticia Miranda and Caitlin Fichtel, "As the Overall Job Market Stumbles Back, Women Still Struggle to Recover Lost Employment," NBC News, May 7, 2021, https://www.nbcnews.com/business/economy/overall-job-market-stumbles-back-women-still-struggle-recover-lost-n1266644.

55 *plummeting birthrate in this country:* Mike Stobbe, "US Birth Rate Falls to Lowest Point in More Than a Century," *US News & World Report*, May 5, 2021, https://www.usnews.com/news/us/articles/2021-05-05/us-birth-rate-falls-to-lowest-point-in-more-than-a-century.

56 *replace themselves without immigration:* Melissa S. Kearney and Phillip Levine, "Will Births in the US Rebound? Probably Not," Brookings, May 24, 2021, https://www.brookings.edu/blog/up-front/2021/05/24/will-births-in-the-us-rebound-probably-not/.

56 *women were on track to make up a majority:* Richard Fry, "U.S.

Women Near Milestone in the College-Educated Labor Force,"
Pew Research Center, June 20, 2019, https://www.pewresearch
.org/fact-tank/2019/06/20/u-s-women-near-milestone-in-the
-college-educated-labor-force/.

56 *innovation is* six times higher: Ellyn Shook, and Julie Sweet,
"Equality = Innovation: Getting to Equal 2019: Creating a Cul-
ture That Drives Innovation," Accenture Research, 2019, https://
www.accenture.com/_acnmedia/Thought-Leadership-Assets/PDF
/Accenture-Equality-Equals-Innovation-Gender-Equality-Research
-Report-IWD-2019.pdf#zoom=50, accessed October 2021.

57 *at risk for mental health and substance abuse disorders:* Myrna M.
Weissman, Priya Wickramaratne, Yoko Nomura, Virginia Warner,
Daniel Pilowsky, and Helen Verdeli, "Offspring of Depressed
Parents: 20 Years Later," *The American Journal of Psychiatry* 163: 6
(2006), https://pubmed.ncbi.nlm.nih.gov/16741200/.

Chapter 3: From Rosie the Riveter to #Girlboss

62 *The first generation of college-educated women:* Gale Encyclopedia of
U.S. Economic History, s.v. "Women in the Workplace," https://
www.encyclopedia.com/history/encyclopedias-almanacs-tran
scripts-and-maps/women-workplace-issue, accessed October 2021.

65 *all the opportunities and advantages of life:* "The Ballot—Bread, Vir-
tue, Power," *The Revolution,* January 8, 1868, Vol. 1, No. 1 edition.

66 *to close the wage gap:* Betty Friedan, "The National Organization
for Women's 1966 Statement of Purpose," National Organization
for Women, October 29, 1966, https://now.org/about/history
/statement-of-purpose/.

66 *women working outside the home:* Emily Seamone, "Women and
Work in the 1970s," *Women, Work, and Life,* July 30, 2014, http:
//www.womenworklife.com/2014/07/30/work-life-really-like
-women-1970s/, accessed October 2021.

67 *simple and revolutionary:* Sarah Jaffe, "The Factory in the Family," *The Nation,* March 14, 2018, https://www.thenation.com
/article/archive/wages-for-houseworks-radical-vision/.

Chapter 4: The Counternarrative: Women at Home

78 *a competitive sport:* Kim Brooks, "Parenting Has Become a Competitive Sport Rather Than a Communal Responsibility," *The Globe and Mail*, August 24, 2018, https://www.theglobeandmail.com /opinion/article-parenting-has-become-a-competitive-sport-rather -than-a-communal/.

79 *doubled since the early 1980s:* "Today's Parents Spend More Time with Their Kids Than Moms and Dads Did 50 Years Ago," UCI News, September 28, 2016, https://news.uci.edu/2016/09/28 /todays-parents-spend-more-time-with-their-kids-than-moms -and-dads-did-50-years-ago.

81 *"And because the enemies should be allies":* "Mommy vs. Mommy," *Newsweek,* June 3, 1990, https://www.newsweek.com/mommy-vs -mommy-206132.

82 *"the stereotype of the ideal mother":* Kim A. Weeden, Youngjoo Cha, and Mauricio Bucca, "Long Work Hours, Part-Time Work, and Trends in the Gender Gap in Pay, the Motherhood Wage Penalty, and the Fatherhood Wage Premium," *The Russell Sage Foundation Journal of the Social Sciences* 2: 4 (2016), https://muse .jhu.edu/article/630321.

Chapter 5: The Four Forces of Change

91 *fully and without distraction:* Joan C. Williams, "The Pandemic Has Exposed the Fallacy of the 'Ideal Worker'," *Harvard Business Review,* May 11, 2020, https://hbr.org/2020/05/the-pandemic -has-exposed-the-fallacy-of-the-ideal-worker.

Chapter 6: EMPOWER: Changing Our Reality from Within

95 *staying sane and in fabulous shape:* Anne-Marie Slaughter, "Why Women Still Can't Have It All," *The Atlantic,* July 2012, https: //www.theatlantic.com/magazine/archive/2012/07/why-women -still-cant-have-it-all/309020/.

98 *negative outcomes of our decisions:* Vinod Venkatraman, Lisa

Chuah, Scott A. Huettel, and Michael W. L. Chee, "Sleep Deprivation Elevates Expectation of Gains and Attenuates Response to Losses Following Risky Decisions," *Sleep* 30 (5), May 2007, https://doi.org/10.1093/sleep/30.5.603.

98 *Sleep deprivation is directly linked:* Anabel Bejarano, "Self Care for Women: Now Not Later," APA Convention, 2008, https://www .apa.org/education-career/development/early/self-care.pdf.

98 *impaired immunity:* "Here's What Happens When You Don't Get Enough Sleep (And How Much You Really Need a Night)," Cleveland Clinic HealthEssentials, June 16, 2020, https://health .clevelandclinic.org/happens-body-dont-get-enough-sleep/.

99 *women prioritize the management of healthcare:* Vera Sizensky, "New Survey: Moms Are Putting Their Health Last," HealthyWoman, March 27, 2015, https://www.healthywomen.org/content/article /new-survey-moms-are-putting-their-health-last.

100 *looking after their family came before:* Karen Gordon, "Growing Number of Women Ignoring Potentially Life-Threatening Symptoms," Netdoctor, February 29, 2016, https://www .netdoctor.co.uk/healthy-living/wellbeing/news/a26199 /women-ignoring-life-threatening-symptoms/.

100 *self-care gets put on the back burner:* Kaitlyn Pirie, "How Amy Klobuchar's Breast Cancer Diagnosis Inspired Her Fight for New Legislation," *Prevention*, November 5, 2021, https://www.prevention .com/health/a38105552/preventive-care-awareness-act/.

102 *$4.2 trillion:* "Wellness Industry Statistics & Facts," Global Wellness Institute, October 2018, https://globalwellnessinstitute.org /press-room/statistics-and-facts/.

102 *doubled since 2015:* Google Trends, s.v. "self-care," accessed November 13, 2021, https://trends.google.com/trends/explore?q =self-care&geo=US.

102 *improve concentration and sharpen cognition:* Matthew Glowiak, "What Is Self-Care and Why Is It Important for You?," Southern New Hampshire University, April 14, 2020, https://www .snhu.edu/about-us/newsroom/health/what-is-self-care.

102　*everything from resilience to weight loss:* John Hall, "Self-Care Isn't Just Good for You—It's Also Good for Your Productivity," *Forbes,* January 5, 2020, https://www.forbes.com/sites/johnhall/2020/01/05/self-care-isnt-just-good-for-you-its-also-good-for-your-productivity/?sh=2974fd2219ff.

103　*higher levels of stress:* David Rock, "A Sense of Autonomy Is a Primary Reward or Threat for the Brain," *Psychology Today,* November 8, 2009, https://www.psychologytoday.com/us/blog/your-brain-work/200911/sense-autonomy-is-primary-reward-or-threat-the-brain.

106　*increased rates of suicide:* Amelia Harnish, "Why Perfectionism Could Be Killing You," *Health,* October 3, 2014, https://www.health.com/condition/depression/why-perfectionism-could-be-killing-you.

109　*lower levels of pain intensity:* Meghan G. Schinkel, Christine T. Chambers, Line Caes, and Erin C. Moon, "A Comparison of Maternal versus Paternal Nonverbal Behavior during Child Pain," *Pain Practice* 17: 1 (2016), https://doi.org/10.1111/papr.12415.

Chapter 7: EDUCATE: Reimagining the Workplace

115　*discussed the need for paid time off and subsidized childcare:* Rob Peters, "Child Care Crisis a Hot Topic for Public Companies and Workforce," Intelligize.com, August 13, 2020, https://www.intelligize.com/child-care-crisis-a-hot-topic-for-public-companies-and-workforce/, accessed October 2021.

117　*also want flexibility:* "Employees Value Flexibility Over Salary Increases—One-Third Looking for New Jobs," Grant Thornton LLP, October 6, 2021, https://www.grantthornton.com/library/press-releases/2021/october/gt-survey-employees-value-flexibility-over-salary-increases-one-third-looking-for-new-jobs.aspx.

118　*hybrid working arrangements:* Susan Lund, Anu Madgavkar, James Manyika, Sven Smit, Kweilin Ellingrud, and Olivia Robinson, "The Future of Work After COVID-19," McKinsey & Company,

February 18, 2021, https://www.mckinsey.com/featured-insights
/future-of-work/the-future-of-work-after-covid-19.

118 *healthy lifestyle behaviors:* Helen Pluut and Jaap Wonders, "Not
Able to Lead a Healthy Life When You Need It the Most: Dual
Role of Lifestyle Behaviors in the Association of Blurred Work-
Life Boundaries with Well-Being," *Frontiers in Psychology* 11,
December 2020, https://doi.org/10.3389/fpsyg.2020.607294.

118 *that "perk" can have a hidden downside:* Lane C. Powell, "Flexible
Scheduling and Gender Equality: The Working Families Flexibility Act Under the Fourteenth Amendment," *Michigan Journal
of Gender & Law* 20 (2), 2013, https://core.ac.uk/download
/pdf/232689296.pdf.

118 *fifty percent reduced rate of promotion:* Nicholas Bloom, James
Liang, John Roberts, and Zhichun Jenny Ying, "Does Working
from Home Work? Evidence from a Chinese Experiment," *The
Quarterly Journal of Economics* 130: 1 (2015), https://academic
.oup.com/qje/article/130/1/165/2337855?searchresult=1.

120 *the location of their choice:* Laurence Goasduff, "Digital Workers
Say Flexibility Is Key to Their Productivity," Gartner.com, June
9, 2021, https://www.gartner.com/smarterwithgartner/digital
-workers-say-flexibility-is-key-to-their-productivity, accessed
October, 2021.

120 *some sort of flexibility:* "More Than Half of Employees Globally
Would Quit Their Jobs If Not Provided Post-Pandemic Flexibility, EY Survey Finds," EY Global, May 12, 2021, https://www
.ey.com/en_gl/news/2021/05/more-than-half-of-employees
-globally-would-quit-their-jobs-if-not-provided-post-pandemic
-flexibility-ey-survey-finds, accessed October 2021.

121 *Only four percent:* "High Performance Flexible Work Culture:
Success Depends on Strategy and Training," Flex Strategy Group,
2018, https://flexstrategygroup.com/wp-content/uploads
/2018/08/FlexStrategyGroupReportUpdateAug2018-1.pdf,
accessed October 2021.

122 *allowing the associate the stability to plan their life:* Matt Smith,

"New Scheduling System Gives Associates More Consistency and Flexibility," Walmart.com, 2018, https://corporate.walmart.com/newsroom/2018/11/13/new-scheduling-system-gives-associates-more-consistency-and-flexibility, accessed October 2021.

123 *childcare was unaffordable:* Katie Reilly and Belinda Luscombe, "Why Affordable Childcare Is Out of Reach for So Many People," *Time*, 2020, https://time.com/child-care-crisis/.

123 *the highest percentage in the world:* Stephanie Kramer, "U.S. Has World's Highest Rate of Children Living in Single-Parent Households," Pew Research Center, December 12, 2019, https://www.pewresearch.org/fact-tank/2019/12/12/u-s-children-more-likely-than-children-in-other-countries-to-live-with-just-one-parent/.

123 *up to thirty-seven percent:* "The US and the High Cost of Child Care," Child Care Aware of America, 2021, https://cdn2.hubspot.net/hubfs/3957809/COCreport2018_1.pdf?__hstc=122076244.ac5e4ad3da743320619f815.

124 *Only one percent:* Joann S. Lublin, "Mothers Are Postponing the Return to Work. Amazon and Other Companies Are Trying to Bring Them Back," *The Wall Street Journal*, September 23, 2021, https://www.wsj.com/articles/mothers-delay-workplace-return-11632331364?mod=Searchresults_pos3&page=1.

125 *sixty-seven percent of companies:* "Benefits by the Numbers: Companies Offering HSAs, FSAs, and HRAs in 2018," Connect Your Care, 2019, https://www.connectyourcare.com/blog/benefits-numbers-companies-offering-cdhp-hsa-fsa-hra-2018/, accessed October 2021.

126 *two times an employee's annual salary:* Shane McFeely and Ben Wigert, "This Fixable Problem Costs U.S. Businesses $1 Trillion," Gallup, March 13, 2019, https://www.gallup.com/workplace/247391/fixable-problem-costs-businesses-trillion.aspx.

126 *women on average do fifty percent more:* Devan McGuinness, "Women Spend 50 Percent More Time Providing Care Than

Men," *Fatherly,* June 7, 2021, https://www.fatherly.com/news
/study-caregiving-men-women/.

126 *two hours more per day:* Drew Weisholtz, "Women Do 2 More
Hours of Housework Daily Than Men, Study Says," *TODAY,*
January 22, 2020, https://www.today.com/news/women-do-2
-more-hours-housework-daily-men-study-says-t172272.

127 *respected field in which men dominate:* "Chefs & Head Cooks,"
Data USA, 2020, https://datausa.io/profile/soc/chefs-head
-cooks, accessed October 2021.

127 *the ones who most often prepare the meals:* Katherine Schaeffer,
"Among U.S. Couples, Women Do More Cooking and Grocery
Shopping Than Men," Pew Research Center, September 24,
2019, https://www.pewresearch.org/fact-tank/2019/09/24
/among-u-s-couples-women-do-more-cooking-and-grocery
-shopping-than-men/.

128 *ninety percent of the employees:* "The Economics of Child Care
Supply in the United States," U.S. Department of the Treasury,
September 2021, https://home.treasury.gov/system/files/136
/The-Economics-of-Childcare-Supply-09-14-final.pdf.

128 *seventy-three percent are people of color:* "Playing Dirty," Unite Here,
2021, https://unitehere.org/wp-content/uploads/Playing-Dirty
-Report-FINAL.pdf.

132 *"challenge traditional assumptions":* Danone North America,
"Danone Expands Parental Leave to 3,500 Manufacturing Colleagues, Promoting Gender Equity for All," Cision PR Newswire,
December 1, 2020, https://www.prnewswire.com/news-releases
/danone-expands-parental-leave-to-3-500-manufacturing
-colleagues-promoting-gender-equity-for-all-301182120.html,
accessed October 2021.

132 *less than half of men:* Francesca Colantuoni, Wahi Diome-Deer,
Karl Moore, Shaibyaa Rajbhandari, and Gila Tolub, "A Fresh
Look at Paternity Leave: Why the Benefits Extend Beyond the
Personal," McKinsey & Company, March 5, 2021, https://www
.mckinsey.com/business-functions/people-and-organizational

-performance/our-insights/a-fresh-look-at-paternity-leave-why
-the-benefits-extend-beyond-the-personal, accessed October
2021.

132 *a woman's income rose 6.7 percent for every month:* Elly-Ann Jo-
hansson, "The Effect of Own and Spousal Parental Leave on
Earnings," The Institute for Labour Market Policy Evaluation,
March 22, 2010, https://www.econstor.eu/bitstream/10419
/45782/1/623752174.pdf.

132 *the hormones responsible for stimulating breastmilk:* Julia Dennison,
"Why New Dads Should Take Paternity Leave," *Parents,* https:
//www.parents.com/pregnancy/my-life/maternity-paternity
-leave/why-new-dads-should-take-paternity-leave/.

133 *not a bad skill to have:* Ibid.

133 *higher cognitive test scores:* "Paternity Leave: Why Parental Leave for
Fathers Is So Important for Working Families," Department of
Labor policy brief, https://www.dol.gov/sites/dolgov/files/OASP
/legacy/files/PaternityBrief.pdf.

133 *higher satisfaction with parenting:* Ibid.

135 *five times more likely:* Usha Ranji, and Alina Salganicoff, "Data
Note: Balancing on Shaky Ground: Women, Work and Family
Health," Kaiser Family Foundation, October 20, 2014, https:
//www.kff.org/womens-health-policy/issue-brief/data-note
-balancing-on-shaky-ground-women-work-and-family-health/.

135 *caregiving roles for elderly parents at home:* Nidhi Sharma, Subho
Chakrabarti, and Sandeep Grover, "Gender Differences in
Caregiving Among Family—Caregivers of People with Mental Illnesses," *World Journal of Psychiatry* 6 (1), March 22, 2016,
10.5498/wjp.v6.i1.7.

137 *more likely to go to work while sick:* Stefen Pichler, Katherine Wen,
and Nicolas R. Ziebarth, "COVID-19 Emergency Sick Leave
Has Helped Flatten the Curve in the United States," *Health-
Affairs* 39: 12 (October 15, 2020), https://www.healthaffairs.org
/doi/10.1377/hlthaff.2020.00863.

138 *viewed as less dependable:* Shelley J. Correll, Stephen Benard, and

In Paik, "Getting a Job: Is There a Motherhood Penalty?" *American Journal of Sociology* 112: 5 (March 2007), https://sociology .stanford.edu/sites/g/files/sbiybj9501/f/publications/getting _a_job-_is_there_a_motherhood_penalty.pdf.

139 *twice as likely to be asked:* Ibid.

139 *disrespectful or "othering" behaviors:* Alexis Krivkovich, Irina Starikova, Kelsey Robinson, Rachel Valentino, and Lareina Yee, "Women in the Workplace 2021," McKinsey, September 27, 2021, https://www.mckinsey.com/featured-insights/diversity -and-inclusion/women-in-the-workplace.

139 *a phenomenon known as "downshifting":* Amanda Hindlian, Sandra Lawson, Sonya Banerjee, Deborah Mirabel, Hui Shan, and Emma Campbell-Mohn, "Closing the Gender Gaps: Advancing Women in Corporate America," Goldman Sachs, 2018, https: //www.goldmansachs.com/insights/pages/gender-pay-gap-f /gmi-gender-gaps.pdf.

140 *much of the gender pay gap:* Claire Cain Miller, "The Gender Pay Gap Is Largely Because of Motherhood," *The New York Times*, May 13, 2017, https://www.nytimes.com/2017/05/13/upshot /the-gender-pay-gap-is-largely-because-of-motherhood.html.

140 *an eighteen percent penalty:* Julie Kashen and Jessica Milli, "The Build Back Better Plan Would Reduce the Motherhood Penalty," The Century Foundation, October 8, 2021, https://tcf.org /content/report/build-back-better-plan-reduce-motherhood -penalty/?agreed=1.

140 *greater than the pay gap between men and women:* Shelley J. Correll, Stephen Benard, and In Paik, "Getting a Job: Is There a Motherhood Penalty?" *American Journal of Sociology* 112: 5 (March 2007), https://sociology.stanford.edu/sites/g/files/sbiybj9501/f /publications/getting_a_job-_is_there_a_motherhood_penalty .pdf.

140 *decrease the motherhood penalty:* Julie Kashen and Jessica Milli, "The Build Back Better Plan Would Reduce the Motherhood Penalty," The Century Foundation, October 8, 2021, https://tcf

.org/content/report/build-back-better-plan-reduce-motherhood
-penalty/?agreed=1.

142 *twenty weeks of paid leave:* Marguerite Ward, "10 Countries
That Show Just How Behind the US Is in Paid Parental Leave
for New Mothers and Fathers," *Business Insider,* May 5, 2020,
https://www.businessinsider.com/countries-with-best-parental
-leave-2016-8#serbia-6.

144 *miscarry or have a stillbirth:* Kimberly Langdon MD, ed., "Postpartum Depression Statistics," Postpartum Depression, June 3, 2021,
https://www.postpartumdepression.org/resources/statistics/,
accessed October 2021.

144 *reduced infant mortality rate:* "The Child Development Case for
a National Paid Family and Medical Leave Program," Zero to
Three, December 17, 2018, https://www.zerotothree.org
/resources/204-the-child-development-case-for-a-national
-paid-family-and-medical-leave-program, accessed October
2021.

145 *ninety-three percent*: "Rutgers Study Finds Paid Family Leave
Leads to Positive Economic Outcomes," *Rutgers Today,* January
19, 2021, https://www.rutgers.edu/news/rutgers-study-finds
-paid-family-leave-leads-positive-economic-outcomes, accessed
October 2021.

145 *more than three-fourths of workers:* "Paid Family Leave Adds Value
to Both Companies and Employees," Consultancy.uk, February
17, 2017, https://www.consultancy.uk/news/13080/paid-family
-leave-adds-value-to-both-companies-and-employees, accessed
October 2021.

145 *greater positive outcomes in profitability*: Eileen Appelbaum and
Ruth Milkman, "Paid Family Leave Pays Off in California," *Harvard Business Review,* January 19, 2011, https://hbr.org/2011/01
/paid-family-leave-pays-off-in.

147 *companies will offer returnships*: Joann S. Lublin, "Mothers Are
Postponing the Return to Work. Amazon and Other Companies Are Trying to Bring Them Back," *The Wall Street Journal,*

September 23, 2021, https://www.wsj.com/articles/mothers
-delay-workplace-return-11632331364.

149 *"It's a New Era for Mental Health at Work"*: Kelly Greenwood and
Julia Anas, "It's a New Era for Mental Health at Work," *Harvard
Business Review,* October 4, 2021, https://hbr.org/2021/10/its
-a-new-era-for-mental-health-at-work.

150 *high demands and pressure:* "Workplace Stress," American Psy-
chiatric Association Foundation Center for Workplace Mental
Health, https://workplacementalhealth.org/Mental-Health
-Topics/Workplace-Stress, accessed October 2021.

150 *stress and burnout:* Ashley Powdar, "How to Bridge the Equity
Gaps in a Hybrid Workforce," AARP, September 8, 2021,
https://www.aarp.org/work/employers/info-2021/hybrid
-workforce-equity.html.

151 *a twentyfold increase in employees' likelihood to stay:* "Parents at the
Best Workplaces: The Largest-Ever Study of Working Parents,"
Maven, 2020, https://info.mavenclinic.com/pdf/parents-at
-the-best-workplaces?submissionGuid=5ac95855-8079-46ac
-9ba5-f8b11c2ae5c5.

154 *increased productivity and economic gains:* "Mental Health in the
Workplace," World Health Organization, accessed November
2021, https://www.who.int/teams/mental-health-and-substance
-use/promotion-prevention/mental-health-in-the-workplace.

155 *lack of productivity:* Monique Valcour, "Beating Burnout," *Harvard Business Review,* November 2016, https://hbr.org/2016/11
/beating-burnout.

156 *increased priority for business leaders:* "The Next Normal: Tomorrow's Workforce in Focus," Randstad, accessed November 2021,
https://rlc.randstadusa.com/for-business/learning-center
/future-workplace-trends/next-normal-workforce-trends.

Chapter 8: REVISE: Shifting the Narrative in Our Culture

162 *children and family lives will suffer:* Catherine Verniers and Jorge
Vala, "Justifying Gender Discrimination in the Workplace:

The Mediating Role of Motherhood Myths," *PLOS ONE* 13: 1, January 9, 2018, https://journals.plos.org/plosone/article ?id=10.1371/journal.pone.0190657.

163 *"more powerful positions"*: Sreedhari D. Desai, Dolly Chugh, and Arthur Brief, "The Organizational Implications of a Traditional Marriage: Can a Domestic Traditionalist by Night Be an Organizational Egalitarian by Day?," *SSRN Electronic Journal*, 2012, https://doi.org/10.2139/ssrn.2018259.

165 *"drink a glass of rosé"*: Monica Hesse, "Perspective: The Unreasonable Expectations of American Motherhood," *The Washington Post*, June 15, 2021, https://www.washingtonpost.com/lifestyle /style/birth-rate-american-mothers/2021/06/14/045c4684 -c950-11eb-81b1-34796c7393af_story.html.

Chapter 9: ADVOCATE: From Rage to Power

170 *"without harm or barriers"*: Amanda Svachula, "From 'SHEcession' to 'SHEcovery': How We Can Bring Women Back into the Workplace," *Katie Couric*, February 23, 2021, https://katiecouric.com /culture/op-ed-from-shecession-to-shecovery-how-we-can-bring -women-back-into-the-workplace/.

172 *almost double what they pay:* Jason DeParle, "When Child Care Costs Twice as Much as the Mortgage," *The New York Times*, October 9, 2021, https://www.nytimes.com/2021/10/09/us /politics/child-care-costs-wages-legislation.html.

172 *seeking quality childcare:* Cristina Novoa, "How Child Care Disruptions Hurt Parents of Color Most," The Center for American Progress, June 29, 2020, https://www.americanprogress .org/article/child-care-disruptions-hurt-parents-color.

173 *Black mothers are more likely:* Jessica Washington, " 'One Paycheck Away from Losing Everything': Why the Child Care Crisis Is Especially Hard for Black Mothers," The Fuller Project, August 25, 2021, https://fullerproject.org/story/child-care-crisis-black -mothers-covid-pandemic-economy/.

173 *public assistance or a second job:* Megan Leonhardt, "Many Child-

Care Workers Don't Earn a Living Wage—and That Was the Case Even Before the Pandemic," CNBC, February 24, 2021, https://www.cnbc.com/2021/02/24/child-care-workers-among -the-one-of-the-lowest-paid-occupations.html.

173 *below the current federal poverty level:* Linda Smith, Kathlyn McHenry, Maya Jasinska, and Rachel Fu, "Minimum Wage Increases: Impacts for Child Care Workers and Providers," Bipartisan Policy Center, June 23, 2021, https://bipartisanpolicy .org/blog/minimum-wage-increases-child-care/, accessed October 2021.

174 *"Childcare is the work that enables":* Rasheed Malik, "Growing the Economy Through Affordable Child Care," The Center for American Progress, May 24, 2021, https://www.american progress.org/issues/early-childhood/reports/2021/05/24 /499825/growing-economy-affordable-child-care/.

175 *less burden on the healthcare industry:* "The Economics of Child Care Supply in the United States," U.S. Department of the Treasury, September 2021, https://home.treasury.gov/system /files/136/The-Economics-of-Childcare-Supply-09-14-final.pdf.

175 *equal to that of women in Norway:* Cynthia Koons, "The U.S. Child-Care Crisis Is Torturing Parents and the Economy," *Bloomberg,* December 10, 2020, https://www.bloomberg.com /news/articles/2020-12-10/u-s-economy-could-get-a-boost-from -expanded-child-care.

175 *eighty-five percent of the cost:* Claire Cain Miller, "How Other Nations Pay for Child Care. The U.S. Is an Outlier," *The New York Times,* October 6, 2021, https://www.nytimes.com/2021/10/06 /upshot/child-care-biden.html.

176 *our youngest and most vulnerable:* Ari Shapiro, "How Politics Killed Universal Child Care in the 1970s," NPR, October 13, 2016, https://www.npr.org/transcripts/497850292.

176 *first four years of a child's life:* First Five Years Fund, "Why It Matters," https://www.ffyf.org/why-it-matters/, accessed October 2021.

179   *saw the attrition rate go down:* Claire Cain Miller, "Paid Leave Encourages Female Employees to Stay," *The New York Times,* July 28, 2014, https://www.nytimes.com/2014/07/29/upshot /how-paid-leave-helps-female-employees-stay-.html.

179   *costs working families:* U.S. Congress, *House, Family and Medical Insurance Leave (FAMILY ACT) Act of 2019,* H.R.1185, 116th Cong, https://www.congress.gov/bill/116th-congress/house-bill /1185/text.

179   *forty percent more likely to require public assistance:* U.S. Congress, *The Economic Benefits of Paid Leave: Fact Sheet,* Joint Economic Committee of the United States Congress, https://www.jec .senate.gov/public/_cache/files/646d2340-dcd4-4614-ada9 -be5b1c3f445c/jec-fact-sheet---economic-benefits-of-paid-leave .pdf.

181   *eleven wealthy countries:* Dylan Matthews, "Sweden Pays Parents for Having Kids—and It Reaps Huge Benefits. Why Doesn't the US?" *Vox,* May 23, 2016, https://www.vox.com/2016/5/23 /11440638/child-benefit-child-allowance.

183   *decrease driving deaths by fifty-five percent:* MADD, "History," https://www.madd.org/history, accessed October 2021.

183   *millions of moms:* Erin Delmore, "This Is How Women Voters Decided the 2020 Election," NBC News, November 13, 2020, https://www.nbcnews.com/know-your-value/feature/how -women-voters-decided-2020-election-ncna1247746.

To access the index, please visit:
https://www.simonandschuster.com/books
/Pay-Up/Reshma-Saujani/9781982191573

For additional information about Pay Up *or other*
works by Reshma Saujani, please visit:
https://reshmasaujani.com

About the Author

Reshma Saujani is a leading activist and the founder of Girls Who Code and the Marshall Plan for Moms. She has spent more than a decade advocating for women and girls' economic empowerment, working to close the gender gap in the tech sector, and, most recently, championing policies to support mothers impacted by the pandemic. Saujani is also the author of the international bestseller *Brave, Not Perfect*, and her influential TED Talk, "Teach Girls Bravery, Not Perfection," has more than five million views across multiple platforms. She lives in New York City with her husband, Nihal; their sons, Shaan and Sai; and their bulldog, Stanley.